THE
CRITICAL
FIRST YEARS
OF YOUR
PROFESSIONAL
LIFE

THE
CRITICAL
FIRST YEARS
OF YOUR
PROFESSIONAL
LIFE

ROBERT L. DILENSCHNEIDER
with Mary Jane Genova

CITADEL PRESS
Kensington Publishing Corp.
www.kensingtonbooks.com

CITADEL PRESS E-BOOKS are published by

Kensington Publishing Corp.
119 West 40th Street
New York, NY 10018

All Kensington titles, imprints, and distributed lines are available at special quantity discounts for bulk purchases for sales promotions, premiums, fund-raising, educational, or institutional use. Special book excerpts or customized printings can also be created to fit specific needs. For details, write or phone the office of the Kensington special sales manager: Kensington Publishing Corp., 119 West 40th Street, New York, NY 10018, attn: Special Sales Department; phone 1-800-221-2647.

First electronic edition: January 2014

ISBN-13: 978-0-8065-3676-7
ISBN-10: 0-8065-3676-4

First printing: January 2014

10 9 8 7 6 5 4 3 2

ISBN-13: 978-0-8065-3677-4
ISBN-10: 0-8065-3677-2

Printed in the United States of America

Library of Congress Cataloging-in-Publication data is available.

To the American worker,
who will continue to drive the USA forward
in a challenging global environment

CONTENTS

ACKNOWLEDGMENTS

The idea for this book arose when unemployment in the United States grew beyond 10 percent. That figure, large as it was, underrepresented the situation. The actual number of men and women out of work exceeded 17 percent, because the official count, as issued by the US Bureau of Labor Statistics, did not include people who had given up looking for jobs. So the problem was worse than it appeared to be.

The same is true today. It's tough out there, and young people who are trying to launch their careers are struggling to do so. That's why the time seems right for a new edition of *The Critical First Years of Your Professional Life*. When it was originally published in 1997, it helped thousands of young people. I believe it has the potential to do so again. Michaela Hamilton, editor in chief of Citadel Press, agrees. Without her encouragement and assistance, this project would not have come to fruition.

I want to thank Jean Allen, Orlando Camargo, Stephen Greyser, Astro Teller, and Sheila Wellington, each of whom graciously agreed to be interviewed for this book.

Nancy Hathaway, my frequent collaborator, joined with me to update the original manuscript.

My wife, Jan, continues to provide a level of support and inspiration that is uncommon. It would be difficult for me to undertake any project like this without her patience, advice, and counsel.

Finally, no page of acknowledgments would be complete without highlighting the support of Joan Avagliano, who has worked with me for more than two decades. Her assistance on this book—and, indeed, all the work we do together—has been invaluable, ranging from formation of strategy to completion of the finest detail.

To all these people I am so grateful.

FOREWORD

Starting off can be tough in any business and at any time. During this age of technological innovation, social media, and remarkable change, it can be downright confusing, especially for young people who are just beginning their careers. Wherever they look, whether at entrepreneurs and their start-ups or at old-line industries, such as health care and banking, that have received makeovers and been given new reach, innovation has changed the game.

Mobility, personal and professional, has dramatically increased. Technology has created new opportunities for advancement in the world of work. It has also encouraged a ready flow of information for billions of people around the world. As one technology executive recently told me, "Having the encyclopedia in your pocket via your cell phone is a really big deal." With all these changes, everything is in flux. Almost every field of business has been affected.

Some have called it the new normal.

Media and entertainment, for example, are being distributed differently than they once were. Banking is being done remotely. Traveling has become more efficient. And changes in technology have enabled numerous improvements in health care. All this, combined with the fact that we are living longer, has created new options and opportunities for all of us. Business has become exciting again.

But embarking on their careers without direction or vision can be treacherous for young people. Business can feel very big, leaving them with a multitude of options and too many questions about whether they have the skill set required to thrive.

Robert Dilenschneider can help. A savvy strategic thinker, he has guided thousands of highly successful people through the worlds of business, the media, academia, politics, and nonprofits. He knows those worlds from the inside, and he has seen the economic, political, and societal changes that have reshaped them.

He also knows that the first years of your professional life, properly managed, will propel you forward for the rest of your career. Bob has shown many how to make the most of these years.

After all, there are so many choices. Should you go the traditional route and try to understand the culture of a big company? Or should you create your own culture with a start-up? *The Critical First Years of Your Professional Life* can help you find the answers to these and many other questions.

The economy is always in motion, and professional life has its own ups and downs. But there are constants to surviving and thriving in your career. Robert L. Dilenschneider has been on the inside for generations, and he knows what those constants are. Whether the economy is weak or strong, he will help you navigate through its changing tides.

—Maria Bartiromo

THE
CRITICAL
FIRST YEARS
OF YOUR
PROFESSIONAL
LIFE

INTRODUCTION

This chapter is must reading IF:

- You're at the start of your career
- You're worried about your professional prospects
- You've just had a big success—and don't want to blow it
- You're stuck at the minimum wage
- You can't seem to get other people to help you with your career

My office is above Grand Central Station, one of the transportation hubs of New York City. So every weekday I see hopeful young men and women, just like you, get off trains and subways and go to their internships and jobs in Manhattan. Most appear determined and sure of themselves. The poignant fact is that some of those young people will make it in their careers, and some of them won't.

Why some young people will succeed and some won't has very little to do with their family backgrounds, the colleges they attended, their majors, the honors they received there, their IQs, their graduate degrees, their athletic skills, or even their ambition and drive.

I can recall a number of young men and women who worked with me in the 1960s who didn't pay attention to learning the ropes. Why didn't they? Some had emotional problems. Some were in the wrong organization and/or the wrong job. Feeling overwhelmed, they shut down and didn't strive to understand how the career game was played. Some were determined to prove that all that mattered was how well they fulfilled their responsibilities. Some were smart alecks who wanted to do it their way. All of them turned out to be under-achievers in the workplace. Despite their backgrounds, brains, and talents, they didn't get anywhere.

To learn the ropes, you first have to admit that you don't have all the answers. Every month I interview bright students for internships and jobs. When it's apparent that they think they have all the answers, I don't invite them back for a second interview. I know that they won't try to figure out the infra-structure of our organization—and that they will flounder.

LEARNING THE ROPES

Success in the workplace depends today, as it did when I was a young man, on one thing: learning the ropes about how the work world operates. For example, if you don't understand how the office grapevine operates, you won't know what to do to correct a negative rumor about yourself. Suppose you've never learned to manage your boss. Then how can you en-courage that boss to help you get where you want to go? Or suppose you can't manage to land that new job or make it into business school in the first place. Do you know what your next steps should be?

THE BRIGHTEST BOY IN THE CLASS

Roger was the thirty-year-old son of one of my clients. His father asked me to talk with Roger about his unstable job his-tory, and so Roger came to see me.

In college Roger had earned a 3.8 grade point average. Since graduation, though, he had experienced one job defeat after an-other, ranging from layoffs to being passed over for promotions. He feared that another layoff was coming, and he wondered what he was doing wrong.

As we talked, I sensed that Roger was the classic case of the bright achiever in college who had difficulty making the tran-sition to the world of work. Because he had done so well in college, he was trying to apply his old techniques for academic success to his jobs.

Thus, as he had in college, Roger would ask provocative questions at work—and, instead of pleasing a professor, would usually irritate his superiors and colleagues. As he had in college, he reflected openly on his feelings and on current events, and, as a result, he made his coworkers uncomfortable. As he had in college, he assumed that his primary responsibility was to do his assignments well; as a result, he simply ignored office politics. In short, after all his efforts in college, Roger hadn't bothered to learn "how to go to work." When I met him, although he had already spent eight years in the workplace, he was still a babe in the woods when it came to knowing what to do day to day on the job.

I gave Roger simple advice: Learn the ropes. Get to know how the workplace operates. Watch what others at work are doing, and figure out why they might be doing it.

I impressed upon him that nearly every act in the workplace is functional. I knew that if he came to understand why certain procedures and traditions existed in the workplace, he could make a choice. He could choose to stay with his current organization and do what he had to do to work within its infrastructure, or he could decide to find a home in an organization whose values were closer to his. Roger opted to move on.

But now he knew that during his first few weeks on his new job he had to figure out the patterns in the organization, or how the place functioned. He turned out to be a quick study. He noticed, for example, that his superiors and coworkers weren't particularly analytical. That told him right away that this was no place to play the "smartest boy in the class." Roger recognized that relationships there were friendly and warm, so he could chat about his feelings and air his opinions on current events. He discerned that office politics revolved around having access to members of the family who owned the organization. Roger made sure he worked out in the gym next to a family member his own age.

THE FIRST YEARS OF YOUR CAREER

Normally, the Rogers of the world and you have a number of years to learn the ropes. What do I mean by "a number"? It varies. But it's probably more than you think it is. In my day, those years generally extended until we were in our early thirties. If you started work immediately after graduation from college at age twenty-one, you might have as long as fourteen years. But things move faster these days and every field is different. So there is no hard-and-fast rule. One point is certain: Those first years may prove to be the most important time in your entire professional career. They are your boot camp: They train you for combat, and you learn how to stay alive in the workplace. You also learn what to do during "peacetime," or when organizational life is proceeding as usual. Think of it as Work 101.

If you don't take full advantage of the opportunity to learn the ropes during those years, you're going to be in trouble. There will be big gaps in your knowledge base, and you won't have developed sound instincts about what to do when and under what circumstances. Without that knowledge base, without those instincts, you'll wind up what I call "work illiterate." This was Roger's situation: During his first eight years in jobs, he simply wasn't interested in learning the ropes.

THESE WILL BE FORGIVING TIMES

Why are those first years so important to your career? Because that's the time slot in which organizations expect you to focus on figuring out how the whole enchilada operates. During that time organizations will be more or less forgiving of your mistakes.

Suppose you work at an advertising agency. Your team is trying to dazzle a client, but you sit there, mute. You don't add any value to the discussion. Afterward, your boss will most likely talk to you about it but probably in an educational, rather than a punitive, way. He'll explain why everyone on the team should speak up in meetings with the client. After his explanation, though, he'll expect you not to make that same mistake again. If you continue to, it may be held against you; it can even become embedded in the organizational memory, and you'll start to develop a bad reputation.

AFTER THE FIRST YEARS

When that initial period ends, you'll definitely be held accountable for what you do and say. There comes a point when you're supposed to "know better." And you will know better— if you've been alert to figuring out the unstated assumptions and infrastructure of the workplace. You'll know when you can go over your boss's head and when you can't. And when you do go over the boss's head, you'll know how to orchestrate it. You will no longer need to rehearse before networking with others. And you will not mistake a bad half year at work for a reason to leave your job.

A GENERATION WITHOUT MENTORS

But there will be a big difference between my experience as a young man starting out in business and your experience. In the 1960s, when I joined a large public relations agency, the world of work was less intense, less competitive, and kinder. On Friday afternoon we could joke around and talk about what we were going to do that weekend. We all knew that if the job didn't work out for any of us at this agency, we could go across the street and get hired by another. But we also knew that if the job did work out, we could stay until we were ready to retire. Gray hair didn't make you a target for the ax back then. There were no periodic purges of staff.

Most important, back then, there were plenty of people on the commuter train into New York City, in the office, in our networks, and even among our clients who were willing to show us the ropes. It didn't feel odd at all to turn to the person in the seat next to me on the train and pour out my heart about whether or not I should accept another job offer. Three-fourths of the people in the office, including most bosses, were my unofficial mentors. At professional meetings such as those of the International Association of Business Communicators, I could always buttonhole people to give me advice on whatever phase of my career I was in. They would even give me their home numbers so I could contact them in the evening.

All those men and women who showed me the ropes during those critical years had the time and inclination to share their wisdom. They weren't working eighteen hours a day in a downsized organization. They weren't trying to become partners in a law firm when there were fewer and fewer partner slots available. Their boss wasn't fired, or their whole department eliminated, soon after they were hired. So, back in the old days, workers tended to be generous with their time and knowledge. And there was a feeling of caring about the next generation. On your first day on the job, a few people would immediately take you under their wing. Today, of course, you young people are often perceived as a threat. To the incumbents you represent people who will work harder than they for less money. As a result, there aren't too many people in your corner right now. And not too many people are showing you the ropes, are they? The current workforce is too busy trying to survive.

On a bad day, whom can you turn to? If I had a bad day at work, I could go to just about anyone at the office and "reverse engineer" that day to figure out what had gone wrong and what I could do about it. I remember the first time a client didn't like my ideas. I was devastated and mortified. When an "elder" at the firm saw me moping around with a long face, he took me aside and unlocked for me the mystery of client relations. He told me that dealing with clients wasn't an exercise in building up my own ego. It was letting clients know that my number one reason for existing was to serve them. And serving them meant that if a certain idea didn't work for them, I would come up with thirty more ideas, and thirty more after that until they were satisfied. From that time on my relationships with clients thrived. I surrendered my ego to their needs. For that I have to thank a forty-year-old gentleman in my office in the 1960s.

For the first several years of my career with that agency, you might say that I had a flock of guardian angels hovering over me. Oh, sure, an occasional person didn't like me. A few lazy old geezers didn't have the energy to help me. And one or two bad apples were out to get me, and, you bet, they gave me bad advice. But, more or less, I was in a cocoon, cared for and protected.

Learning the ropes in those days was relatively painless. And the process worked. After a few years, we were completely socialized to the world of work. I had the system down cold. I could do business in New York City or Moscow, and I knew exactly what to do. I was a "pro."

WHY I WROTE THIS BOOK FOR YOU

Learning the ropes can be equally painless for you. That's why I wrote this book. It substitutes for all those generous men and women who would have helped you in an earlier era. It's the paper or electronic version of a mentor. It's boot camp without having to carry a fifty-pound backpack.

This book contains all the lessons you'll need to learn about functioning at work. To write it, I analyzed my four decades of experience in the work world. I interviewed experts whose opinions you'll find in this book. I did additional research. Most important, I spoke with many of you in person and online. You asked me how to find mentoring in today's workplace. You asked me how not to get discouraged when a good job didn't turn up after you'd pounded the pavement for a year. This book is my answer.

CHAPTER BY CHAPTER

Here are some of the specific things you're going to learn from reading and then thinking about this book.

Chapter 1: How to size up any organizational culture and determine whether you want to become part of it. Maybe you belong at Microsoft instead of Aetna Insurance, or the United Way instead of the Salvation Army. There are so many different organizational cultures today that there's no excuse for being with an organization that's a bad fit for you. Bad fits are career killers.

Chapter 2: How to present yourself during a job search. That includes what to do with "negative" information, such as the job you lost two years ago. The best presenters in interviews, not necessarily the best qualified, get the job. Jean Allen, a partner in Heidrick & Struggles, an international executive search firm, offers the kind of wisdom about the job-search process that only a headhunter can provide.

Chapter 3: Whether you should start your own business. Astro Teller, director of new projects at Google and the founder of several successful small businesses, talks about what it means to be an entrepreneur and offers nuts-and-bolts advice about learning the ropes as a self-employed person.

Chapter 4: How you can manage any boss in any organization. The boss is never your enemy. There are no "bad" bosses. There are only bosses whose needs and wants you haven't yet figured out.

Chapter 5: How to gain access to the office grapevine. Information that comes via the grapevine is vital for you to have. Also, you need to understand how to put information into the grapevine. Remember when the grapevine used to be called "gossip"? Now it's called "survival."

Chapter 6: How to network effectively. Plenty of people are out there exchanging business cards, but most of them aren't getting results. Done right, networking can help you do everything from getting a job to finding a better job, from lining up new business to gathering competitive intelligence. Here you learn how to do all this right. Also, Orlando Camargo, a senior consultant in my own firm and an expert in social media, offers his advice.

Chapter 7: How to make allies of your elders. Older generations hold tremendous power in organizations today, but they often have negative feelings about your generation—and vice versa. Here you learn to replace those negatives with positives.

Chapter 8: How to develop an appropriate image. Your professional image is your trademark, your signature. Here you learn how to shape it and, when necessary, revise it.

Chapter 9: How to have influence at work. For some of you, having influence may seem a dated concept. Wrong. With traditional hierarchies toppling, influence—or the art of getting things done—is more important than ever. In many cases, it's even more important than actual power. Here you'll find out about the wrong and right ways to develop influence.

Chapter 10: What education is all about. Education is an essential part of a professional life. Here you'll look at its purposes and its pitfalls. Stephen Greyser, the Richard P. Chapman Professor of Business Administration (Marketing/Communications) Emeritus at Harvard Business School, offers his views.

Chapter 11: How to balance work and your personal life. The days of the conforming "Organization Man" are over. You're now responsible for making choices about how much personal time you need—and what you're willing to give up for that. Sheila Wellington, Executive-in-Residence at the Leonard N. Stern School of Business at New York University, addresses this and other issues.

Chapter 12: What etiquette you need to know. Since there's been a decline in civility in the workplace and, seemingly, in the world at large, those with good manners often have a competitive advantage. That's primarily because their working relationships are better than those of their colleagues. Bad manners can earn you demerits.

Chapter 13: What to do after a setback. In a volatile economy, we're all encountering more bumps in the road. Here George

Daly, dean of the McDonough School of Business at George-town University, discusses how a crushing blow can be turned into an opportunity. I also discuss my own career setback.

Chapter 14: How to find a mentor. I interview my mentor Wal-ter Seifert, former professor at Ohio State University, who de-scribes how he views the mentor relationship. You'll also get concrete advice on what to expect from a mentor, what your responsibilities are in the relationship, and what to do when you outgrow a mentor.

Chapter 15: How to decide if it's time to change jobs. Sometimes there are valid reasons for leaving a job. This chapter lays out those reasons, with useful tips from headhunter Jean Allen. This is must reading on a bad day.

YOUR PAYOFF: THE FIVE GOALS

What should you get out of this book? This book should give you the tools you'll need to accomplish five goals:

GAINING SELF-KNOWLEDGE

One, you'll find out who you are. When you know who you are, you will be able to evaluate which organizational cultures fit you. If you find the right fit, you have a shot at being happy—even in these crazy economic times. Self-knowledge is the beginning of happiness in the workplace.

When I looked for my first job, I knew myself well enough to realize that I needed a large playing field. I wasn't going to be happy in a mom-and-pop agency in Rye, New York, or do-ing freelance work out of a studio apartment in Manhattan. The right fit for me was a large agency, where there would be lots of clients, lots of meetings at which I could wear my new suits, and lots of room for getting ahead. I found such a place. Had I not found the right fit, my career might have turned out very differently.

FEELING EMPATHY

Two, you'll be more capable of empathy. That is, you'll be better equipped to realize what it feels like to be in another person's shoes—and why that's important. That person might be your boss, colleague, subordinate, supplier, or client. Many mistakes in organizations result from a lack of empathy—the inability to see the world through someone else's eyes.

In discussing success in *Emotional Intelligence,* the best-selling author and psychologist Daniel Goleman stresses the importance of empathy in professional advancement. "People who are empathetic," says Goleman, "are more attuned to the subtle social signals that indicate what others need or want." Those signals help you be on target in your interactions with others.

When I learned to empathize with the pressures my bosses and clients were under, my relationships with them improved 200 percent. Once I understood that my bosses and clients were worried about losing their jobs, their sharp tongues no longer cut me, and I could comprehend the high stakes involved with the project we were working on. So many conflicts in the workplace happen because we are looking inward at ourselves rather than outward at the context we're operating in.

The foundation of empathy is self-knowledge. If you don't understand yourself, you can't understand your fellow creatures.

PRESENTING YOURSELF WELL

Three, you'll be able to present yourself effectively: in person, on the phone, online, and on paper. The world of work has always been based on image. You were hired, or got promoted, for what you seemed to be, not for who you really were. This is more true than ever today. No one in the workplace has the time to find out who the "real you" is. They will select candidates for promotion based on how you appear to them.

In short, you are your image. Presentation skills allow you to shape that image. Often you only have one chance and a few seconds to present yourself. You'd better do it right the first time.

RETRIEVING INFORMATION EFFECTIVELY AND BEING INFORMED

Four, you'll learn how to retrieve information about the organization you work for: its products, its players, its competitors, and so on. Sometimes this will mean knowing how to penetrate the grapevine. Sometimes it will mean knowing how to read a profit-and-loss statement. Often it might require you to find appropriate outside sources for information about your organization. Those outside sources can range from Wall Street security analysts to Bloomberg.com.

The cliché—this is the Information Age—is true. You'd better know how to obtain reliable information on any subject instantaneously. Google is only a starting point.

Beyond that, you will understand how imperative it is to be an informed person, and that's not a goal you can achieve in a single late-night Google session. No matter what field you're in, it is essential to keep up with the news, to know what's happening in the economy, and to understand the challenges facing your particular industry. Whether you plan to spend your career in business or politics, academia or entertainment, the private sector or the public, there is no advantage to ignorance. It will never bring you bliss.

SOLVING PROBLEMS

Five, you will learn how to solve any problem you encounter at work. The big players in organizations are rarely the brightest, most energetic, or most creative. They usually have gotten where they are because they have been superior at solving problems—their own and those of others. And organizations adore problem solvers. It was drummed into me during my first few years of work that I would hang myself if I brought a problem to my superiors. The only appropriate way to deal with a problem in an organization is to approach it from the point of view of possible solutions.

Often, solving a problem involves research. That might mean informally interviewing some information sources. Today, many careers unravel because of a lack of input from the outside. Too many people still try to solve a problem by themselves.

Perhaps the easiest way to learn problem solving is to observe and analyze how others in the organization, particularly the top performers, solve their problems. That way you can learn a tremendous amount tuition-free. It is also important to avoid lapsing into denial. Have you heard that they may downsize your department 45 percent? Don't dismiss the rumor out of hand. Rather, admit there's a problem, and think about strategies for resolving it. Incidentally, staff members are often judged on how well they handle themselves during a downsizing. Another way to learn to problem solve is to make an investment in expert advice. For instance, if you're confused about your job, and all the other methods of solving the recurring problem haven't worked, it might be wise to consult a career counselor.

A SPECIAL GENERATION

When you accomplish those five goals, you're positioned to soar. You can be more successful than any other generation in America's history.

First of all, you're already more pragmatic than any other recent generation has been. The Baby Boomers, for example, largely grew up in a time of affluence and entered the work world when the "Great American Job Machine" was purring. They often became too idealistic and unfocused. But a tough employment market and a challenging global economy have kept your feet firmly on the ground. In the current workplace, that's a trait very much in demand.

Second, you already know that the only thing to do if given a lemon is to make lemonade. Suppose you had a counter job in a fast-food restaurant. Many of you were resourceful enough to turn that experience into something you could leverage both at the restaurant and on your résumé for future jobs. Maybe you worked your way into management at the fast-food establishment, and maybe you got a better job based on that experience. Too often, when the Baby Boomers ran into obstacles, they simply gave up. They weren't adept at turning obstacles into opportunities. You are.

Third, you're wizards in high tech, and you're completely comfortable in the world of social media. Since you're digital natives, it all comes naturally to you. That's a definite plus to bring to any organization.

Fourth, you see through hype. All those hours of watching TV commercials made you discerning. The toy truck advertised on TV filled the screen. But when you ordered it, and the postman brought it to the door, the truck was only about two inches long. You learned not to accept things at face value. You can help your organization be wary of fleeting trends and promises of miracles. You can be the voice of reason.

Fifth, you know that money's important. There was a time when some in the workforce forgot that the number one reason we work is for the paycheck, not self-fulfillment. Organizations want you to have a clear sense of your priorities. And your number one reason for being in the workplace is to earn money. You're not a generation that gets bogged down in abstractions about "expressing yourself," "asserting your creativity," or "changing the world."

WHEN YOU FINISH READING

After you read this book, you're going to have questions. You might wonder if mentors are more bother than they're worth. Is networking really a must? You've seen plenty of ill-mannered colleagues getting promotions. Are manners mandatory?

Those questions are your chance to get talking with one another, with your parents, your colleagues, your subordinates, and even your superiors. **Careers are built primarily on relationships, not expertise.** Focus on your professional relationships, and you'll have access to all the resources you need to get your work done.

Things to Remember

- You have several years to learn the ropes
- Not knowing the ropes puts you at a competitive disadvantage
- Times have changed, and there are fewer people in today's workplace willing to help you understand how the world of work operates
- Professional relationships can give you access to the resources you need

1

GOOD PROFESSIONAL FITS, BAD PROFESSIONAL FITS

This chapter is must reading IF:

- You don't feel comfortable at your organization
- You wonder why certain "types" at your organization keep getting ahead
- You got a job offer, but your instincts say not to take it
- You feel abused at work

My father was a newspaperman. Whenever I run into an ex-newsman in my line of work, I feel an immediate rapport. One day, I was at another public relations agency visiting a friend, who brought me in to see an old newsman I'll call Tim, whom my friend knew I would enjoy meeting.

Well, Tim's office was a pigsty. There were piles of everything everywhere, from candy wrappers to old copies of the *New York Daily News*. While I certainly did feel an emotional rapport, I wondered how Tim was perceived at the agency and by its clients.

After we left Tim's office, my friend started in on the "poor Tims" of the world and how Tim kept getting passed over for promotions. *NEWS FLASH: Tim made a bad impression. He didn't fit in with the buttoned-down organizational culture of the agency. He was never going to get a promotion unless he cleaned up his act—literally—or moved on to a more laid-back organization.*

The work world is filled with "poor Tims" who don't fit in with the organizational culture. Year ago, when many organizations were quite rigid and had little tolerance for individuality, there might have been an explanation for the bad fit. But not now. Organization cultures vary wildly today, from the loose environment of a high-tech start-up to the conservative atmosphere of an old-line bank. It's up to you to find a fit that's right for you. If you wander into the wrong corporate culture, you could be shunned, demoted, passed over for promotion, underestimated, underpaid, and even fired. Organizational life has never been kind to misfits, and it isn't now.

This chapter is an important one. In it you'll learn about good professional fits and bad professional fits. You'll also find out how to differentiate yourself from your colleagues and stand out in an effective way, even as you fit into the organizational culture.

A HOT TOPIC

Organizational culture is a hot topic right now because we have learned that there's a correlation between growth in earnings and a strong organizational culture—one that adapts to changing circumstances, encourages leadership from all levels, and values input from employees, stockholders, and customers. An eleven-year study by John Kotter and James Keskett found that companies with strong organizational cultures increased revenues by 682 percent over that period versus 166 percent for companies with weaker cultures. And the "strong-culture" companies increased their stock prices 901 percent as opposed to 74 percent.

But organizational culture is also a hot topic for another reason. We now realize that to succeed in an organization, you have to fit in with its culture. I remember the days when only tall, white, Anglo-Saxon males could get ahead. We called them "Organization Men." That era is over, but organizations still recruit and promote certain types of people—people who fit well into their organizational culture. Lady Gaga wouldn't have been able to get a job at Citibank, but HP's Meg Whitman could easily have gotten ahead there. Specific organizations are interested in specific types. Organization A may want a very different type of employee than organization B.

WHAT IS ORGANIZATIONAL CULTURE?

What exactly is "organizational culture?" In *Transforming Company Culture,* David Drennan says that organizations have personalities and attitudes. Some banks have stodgy personalities. From the beginning, Microsoft has had an "in your face" attitude. Your challenge is to find an organization that fits with your personality and attitude. Unlike when I was starting my career, there is a lot of diversity out there in how organizations operate. It's possible to find a good fit for yourself no matter who you are, what you look like, or what you value. So there's no excuse for winding up with a bad fit.

Another way of looking at organizational or corporate culture, says Drennan, is analyzing "how things are done around here." That's probably the most useful definition of organizational culture. Everything in an organizational culture has an operational function, including its language, values, procedures, and traditions, no matter how seemingly minor. Coffee breaks serve as an opportunity for networking. An annual picnic can bolster a sense of identification with the company. Free trips to exotic places for salespeople who make their quotas deliver an unmistakable message: *This is the kind of behavior we value.* Humiliating firings deliver a message, too: *This is behavior we don't want at this organization.*

THE MIRACLE AT CHRYSLER

Let's go back in time to one of the strongest cultures in the history of American business. That was the unique culture Lee Iacocca and his turnaround team created in the late 1970s, a culture that helped save a company ready to go belly up. When Iacocca came to Chrysler, the auto company was hemorrhaging red ink. Japanese competition had become a new fact of life. Just down the road was a severe recession that would hurt new car sales badly. At the same time, Chrysler was fighting a public relations battle, trying to tell the nation that the loan guarantees it had received from the US government were justified.

In the late 1970s, most of corporate America was still quite stodgy. Iacocca changed that at Chrysler, and those changes trumpeted the news about the "new" Chrysler. Here are some of the ways Iacocca transformed Chrysler.

- Physically, Chrysler no longer looked like the traditional corporation. To save money, trash collection was cut back, so wastebaskets often overflowed. There was no time to file papers, so piles of paper were all around. The carpet in the executive suite was old and worn. Unlike the case of "poor Tim," or one slovenly individual in a buttoned-down office environment, this overall clutter sent the message that Chrysler was focused on the business, not the cosmetics, of corporate life.
- Iacocca downsized before it became a trend. That told the world, including the government and taxpayers, that Chrysler was serious about getting its cost structure under control.
- Like radicals of the 1960s who staged theater in the streets, the Chrysler turnaround team used drama and entertainment to get their message out to the American public. Iacocca insisted that executives give a certain number of speeches, and those speeches were bold and

candid, very unlike the typical corporate speeches at that time. Because Chrysler's approach to presenting itself was so different, the company got plenty of media attention. That helped sell cars.

• Employees worked long hours, and they bragged rather than complained about that. This work ethic helped Chrysler save money on compensation. To keep its break-even point down, Chrysler had to keep its employee head count down.

• Many meetings, memos, and other traditional corporate procedures were scrapped. More decisions were made in the hallways than in the conference room. This showed the world that Chrysler was serious about cutting costs. It also made employees proud that they were different from all those other complacent companies.

• The pace was fast. This helped communicate the urgency of the situation. It also saved money—since time is money.

Iacocca, a master builder, built an organizational culture that would accomplish what he needed to get done. Across town, Ford Motor Company established an equally effective organizational culture to support their quality mission.

FITTING IN

The most exciting, most effective organizational culture will be irrelevant to your career if you don't fit in with it. In *Built to Last,* James Collins and Jerry Porras observe that the process of trying to make it in strong cultures is binary: Either you fit in, or you are ejected. As I see it, that "either/or" applies to many cultures today, not just strong ones. Downsizing has eliminated many of the corners where people who are bad fits could once hide. As a result, misfits now stand out—and are generally tormented for being different.

THE ELEMENTS OF ORGANIZATIONAL CULTURE

When you apply for a job, much about the organizational culture is right out there for you to see and judge. How the receptionist in the main lobby looks, whether the interviewer offers you a beverage, whether human resources seems suspicious of you: All are clues for decoding the organizational culture.

How do you decide if you'll fit in?

In *Organizational Culture and Leadership,* Edgar Schein presents the eight components of an organizational culture. Let's look at them in terms of you.

1. *Patterns of behavior when people interact.* These include the language, idioms, and jargon people use and the customs, traditions, and rituals they observe. I went to a large computer company in the 1980s looking for business. I noticed that the staff members addressed one another formally and seldom made eye contact. I knew immediately that that wasn't the account for me. Would it put you off if your coworkers were excessively guarded all the time?

Corporate customs tell us a lot about an organization. If the custom is to give all employees stock options, that's a fairly egalitarian company. If the organization still has a tradition of giving turkeys to employees at Thanksgiving, you can assume that the organization tends to be paternalistic and old-line. If there are many rituals at an organization celebrating individual initiative, you can probably conclude that the culture of the organization is a meritocracy where performance is rewarded.

Rituals are always symbolic. They mean something. Once, on a corporate jet, I reached over to get some peanuts from the bar. A hush fell over the group I was traveling with, and I saw the chief executive's administrative assistant turn pale. I looked at the assistant and asked, "Am I doing something wrong?" He said that no one ever ate or drank anything before the CEO did. This observance symbolized the huge importance of the pecking order to that company. If you didn't like a fanatically strict hierarchy, you didn't belong there.

What kind of organization is the best fit for you? There are no perfect fits. But you will be more comfortable in some than in others.

2. *Group norms or unwritten rules.* Organizations usually don't hang up a sign reading THE FOLLOWING STANDARDS AND VALUES ARE WHAT WE'RE ALL ABOUT. Since the rules are primarily unwritten, you have to be alert. You might, for example, suspect that profits are more important than quality at your organization. Listen to how people talk about those two concepts. Do the two seem mutually exclusive? Maybe your mentor or a trusted ally can answer some questions for you.

3. *The espoused or announced values.* Sometimes values are made explicit. These are usually contained in the organization's mission statement or statement of values. This is supposed to tell you what the organization is all about. At Zappos.com, the online shoe store, the official motto is "Powered by Service." They famously take customer service to unprecedented heights. As a result, 75 percent of their sales are to repeat buyers. Focusing on the organization's stated values can help you discover its heartbeat.

4. *Formal philosophy.* This includes the written policies and ideologies that determine how the firm will deal with all its constituencies, from stockholders to employees. This will tell you a lot about the organization. For instance, if the organization has declared that it puts shareholder interests before all else, it might do any number of things—such as downsizing or even selling the company—to boost its stock price. For most of the last century, IBM had a philosophy of not laying off its employees. Because of that policy, security-minded people went to work for IBM even though they might have made more money elsewhere.

5. *"Climate."* If an organization were a restaurant, "climate" would be defined as "ambiance." This includes the physical surroundings and the ways in which people treat one another.

The old-style corporation used to be a large, institutional-type building in which you didn't hang up too many *Dilbert* cartoons. People treated one another cautiously, with outward respect and reserve. Today, if you want, you can find organizations with warm, friendly, and casual climates. People can be quite expressive. Friendships spring up easily. And instead of dressing up, people dress down.

I once applied for a job where the receptionist had the icy look of a model on the cover of *Vogue*. I didn't feel comfortable in that chilly climate and beat a hasty retreat.

6. *Habits of thinking.* At some organizations thinking is done slowly and carefully. There's no jumping to conclusions, and whatever is decided will be reviewed by committees. At other organizations discussion is lively, and employees are ready to take risks. Which one is for you? Problems are solved very differently at the new IBM than they were at the old IBM.

7. *Shared meanings.* At Disney, employees believe that they bring their guests happiness. During the Iacocca turnaround at Chrysler everyone, from executives to security guards, recognized that if they didn't band together to make things work, they could wake up the next morning and their jobs might be gone. Both at Disney and at Chrysler, a shared perception bound the employees together, helping them feel part of something that was bigger than themselves and their individual careers.

8. *Symbolism.* That includes everything from the style of architecture chosen for headquarters to how the building is decorated for the holidays. A consumer products company on the East Coast was housed in an ornate building. When the company was acquired, the new parent company viewed that building as symbolizing all the excesses in the subsidiary's organizational culture.

Many human elements in an organizational culture can also be interpreted symbolically. If human resources and the job interviewer treat you well, that can symbolize the respect the organization has for its human capital.

Whenever I go to visit a new account, I make sure that I see everything symbolically.

YOUR TOP TEN LIST

Many young people tell me they're not sure what they want, so how can they make a decision about their fit with an organizational culture?

The best way to dig down to your inner core is to make a list. On that list write the ten—not eleven, but ten—factors that are most important to you professionally.

Your list might read:

1. A work environment built on trust
2. Interesting work
3. Opportunity to keep learning
4. Respect for the individual
5. Opportunity for good relationships with colleagues
6. Funds available to go toward my MBA at night
7. Good health insurance for my family
8. Regular raises and a bonus system
9. A boss who's not crazy
10. No more than fifty hours a week of work

This list will quickly exclude many organizations, but it also leaves room for compromise. If the organization you're looking at matches most of the items on the list, you might consider it a suitable place for you to go.

CULTURAL CHANGE

As you change and grow, you might need to make a new list. Organizations change, too. Given the importance of corporate culture, many organizations have called in consultants to help them design a culture that will help them work more efficiently. Thus, you might have interviewed at Best Buy and not liked it, but three years later, that organization may have transformed its culture.

What should you do if your organization is changing its culture? I say, sit tight and keep a low profile. You don't want to be too closely identified with either the change agents or the traditionalists. You don't know which faction will triumph. Organizational change requires years of effort, and the change is not always carried out. The "old" regime might fall out of power but then come surging back, undoing everything the new regime implemented.

Of all the roles in an organization, one of the most perilous is to be an agent of change. I know a woman who went to what was then called International Harvester. They paid her well to come in and make some rapid changes. Those changes proved too rapid for the organization. She was fired.

STANDING OUT

Yes, in any organizational culture, it's important to fit in. But you must also stand out by differentiating yourself in positive ways from all the others competing for raises, interesting work, training opportunities, and promotions. An acquaintance, Bob O., learned that the hard way. He was making a decent salary at a radio station, but he wanted more money. He went to his boss and asked for a raise. The boss turned him down. Why? Bob hadn't distinguished himself from all the other voices on the radio. Therefore, as his boss crudely put it, he could hire *another* Bob for less money. Bob had to learn to "add value"—to contribute something unique to the radio station.

No successful person in an organization simply blends in. In a downsized world, that's a quick way to get laid off. If you're not adding value, you're just an expense.

How can you safely stand out? Determine and capitalize on your strengths. Maybe your technical ability or your fluency in a language other than English gives you an edge over your colleagues. Maybe you write killer speeches for the senior executives. Maybe you have keen analytical skills that can help your company save or make more money. Let people know what you're doing, and seek honest feedback on whether you're making a significant contribution. If you're not, find out how you could be more productive or contribute something unique. Also, be sure to keep learning. Seize training opportunities. Maybe you need to take a few classes. Maybe you need an MBA.

As you add value, make sure some of it is public. Many computer geniuses never get anywhere because they don't *leave* their computers.

Find out what others are doing and whether you can help out on their projects. People often get on board with famous projects, such as the Chrysler minivan, by being in the right place at the right time and showing some initiative.

RED ALERT: SEXUAL HARASSMENT

I remember the days when women could do very little about sexual harassment in the workplace. Oftentimes the most they could do—if they dared—was to ask someone with power in the office to tell the turkey to back off. However, times are different. Sexual harassment is no longer tolerated, and the law is finally on the victim's side. Nevertheless, harassers are still out there. When you're investigating an organization, find out if sexual harassment is silently condoned in the culture. (The best sources to ask are former employees.) If you find out that it is, I would steer clear of that place—no matter *what* they offered me.

Things to Remember

- Organizational culture has become very important
- It's not difficult to decode the organizational culture
- Find out what's important to you professionally
- Think twice before you accept the role of change agent
- Differentiate yourself from everyone else in terms of substance, not just style
- Avoid organizations that condone sexual harassment

2

GETTING INSIDE

This chapter on job hunting is must reading IF:

- You're at a pivotal point in your career, and you don't know the next step
- You want to find out how the pros—executives earning $100,000 plus—look for and get jobs
- You need to figure out what you might be doing wrong in your own job search
- You don't know how to sell yourself
- You don't know what questions to ask
- And you want to be happy

Each year literally millions of jobs come on the market. Many of those are good jobs; that is, they pay a living wage, offer decent benefits, and seem as if they could last more than a few years. One of those good jobs should be yours, and you don't have to be a genius (or a miracle worker) to get one. "Normal" people get good jobs every day. What these "normal" people excel at is how they present themselves during a job hunt.

PRESENTING YOURSELF EFFECTIVELY

To get a good job, you have to present yourself in a way that makes you stand out from the competition. In the advertising world, they call this "breaking through the clutter." In your résumé, cover letters, interviewing, and networking, you have to make yourself *memorable.*

It isn't easy. Competition is keen these days. Your résumé might be one of hundreds, all of which have arrived simultaneously in the in-box of an overburdened hiring manager. The only way to catch that person's attention is to distinguish yourself.

You can't do it by presenting your résumé in a fancy font or by having it hand-delivered in a pizza box. A gimmick will not get you in the door. (In fact, it's more likely to have the opposite effect.) What you can do is make sure that you come across as confident, professional, prepared, focused, fully informed about the organization, and excited to work there. This chapter will tell you how.

THE BAD NEWS

Although getting a job was never easy, it's a lot tougher now than it was a few decades ago. Things started changing in the mid-1980s, when America found itself no longer master of the international marketplace. Challenges to our supremacy came from around the globe, particularly from Japan and developing countries. To cope with this competition, US organizations had to cut costs and increase productivity. At the same time, information technology was eliminating much of the need for middle managers and many others. Thus came the great downsizing trauma. Millions of corporate jobs were eliminated, and that belt-tightening had ripple effects in other fields. The 1990s saw an uptick in the economy, and unemployment plummeted. But the dot-com boom was followed by the dot-com bust. Since then, 9/11 and the financial crisis of 2008 have further damaged the economy. Many traditional career paths have disappeared forever.

None of us can ever again assume that we'll have a job for life with a GM or an IBM. Neither can we assume that our income will keep increasing or that our children will be better off than we are. Overtime—and plenty of it—is the new normal. And despite the ease of telecommuting, many employers are demanding that we put in more "face time"—that is, they want us at work for longer hours.

THE GOOD NEWS

If ever there was a generation prepared for tough times, you're it. More educated than previous generations, you are confident, goal-oriented, and ambitious, although you refuse to be defined solely by work and are determined to have a personal life. You have lived through a savage economy and seen raucous political divisiveness, yet, unlike your skeptical colleagues in Generation X, you have high expectations and have maintained optimism. You are the most tolerant, diverse generation in history. Most of all, you have a quality that older people can only gaze upon with awe: You are digital natives, thoroughly at home with technology and, hence, well prepared for the most exciting careers of the future. Even in a period of high unemployment, jobs will be available in nanotechnology, biotech, app development, and virtually every facet of IT. There will be jobs in health care, engineering, and finance. Even in glamour fields such as film and sports management, positions will open up. Somebody will get hired.

All you need is to get one—just one—of those good jobs. But you want that job to be an apt fit with who you really are. Fortunately, the culture of business has changed utterly in the decades since the Organization Man. Today companies do things their own way. And their way may or may not be right for you.

When I was at my previous job, I knew a highly competent

editor of a yachting magazine named Dean Heine. He was doing well and was great to work with. But he wanted to do even better financially. So he joined our large public relations firm. Dean's performance was excellent, but he wasn't happy. It was a bad fit. After three years, he resigned and went back to his first love. It worked for him. He did what made him happy.

Think about your fit with a particular organization and particular job before you accept an offer. Ask yourself these questions:

- Do I like the organization and what it stands for?
- Do I like the people I've met there?
- Do I think that they like me?
- Do I know what I will be doing, and is that something I really want to do?
- Will the job lead to something better? What do I have to do to get to that?
- Do I feel anxious about the job? Or am I happy to have it?

YOUR RÉSUMÉ

Before the work world was turned upside down, having an undergraduate degree from an Ivy League college was generally enough to get you a job. Usually it gained you automatic access to the best organizations. That's no longer the case. The playing field is now more level. We're seeing more of a meritocracy—that is, organizations are rewarding performance and recognizing those who get results.

Back in the 1980s, it was also okay to create a résumé that was chock-full of the facts about your job history. Now a résumé has to do more than give a career history. It has to jump out from the many other résumés submitted in response to the same ad. It has to say, "I'm the one to interview."

How can you make your résumé stand out? Well, you can't send a form letter. And you can't rely on personal contacts. What you have to do is *sell* yourself.

There are simple guidelines for that. Let's look at the "Work History" part of the résumé, where you give details about your professional experience. The best way I've seen to organize this part of a résumé is job by job, starting with your current position. First, state the job title, organization, city, state, and the years you spent at that job.

Next, list your duties, and be specific. If you supervised people, say how many. If you operated equipment, state what kind of equipment it was. If you were part of the product launch team, state how many products were created per year and what the results were.

Third—and this is the most important part—describe your accomplishments. How did your work save time or money or increase profits or quality? You want to *quantify* your accomplishments. For example, you might have been on the Quality Task Force, which improved quality 30 percent and reduced warranty costs by 15 percent. You might have been on the committee that reduced health-care costs by 20 percent. You might have implemented procedures that eliminated 18 percent of paperwork.

Suppose you crated a no-frills newsletter that increased employee readership. You should know by how much—that is, you should have a number you can cite, because numbers talk. But if you don't have those numbers, you can still describe the accomplishment as "Created a reader-friendly newsletter for 1,000 employees in four locations, which increased readership in all locations."

Was your accomplishment a team effort? State that. Put down "Member of the team that created Angry Birds. Sold twelve million copies during the first year."

To come up with a list of accomplishments or results, you may have to go through your typical workday, task by task, and dig to find what impact each of these tasks is having on the bigger picture. Suppose you sort the mail in the customer service department. Your accuracy could be helping to speed up the resolution of customer complaints. Does your department have any numbers on how that turnaround time has been reduced? If there is an accomplishment in your unit, determine if you had a role in it. Ask yourself, "What would have happened had I not sorted the mail correctly?" Connect what you do to the basic functions of the corporation.

Here is a sample entry for the work history.

May 2009—present:	Speechwriter, General Widget, Jersey City, New Jersey
Duties:	Research, write, and edit speeches, articles, blog posts, and reports for senior executives. Liaison with twelve vendors. Responsible for a $50,000 budget.
Accomplishments:	Speeches, articles, and letters written for senior executives appeared in twenty websites and publications ranging from *Vital Speeches of the Day* to the *Wall Street Journal*. Department received one IABC Golden Quill Award and one internal award for quality. Reduced expenses 10 percent.

After your work experience you can have a section labeled "Other Experience" or "Other Skills." Here you can enhance your work record with a description of your volunteer activities. Have you done volunteer work for United Way or the Red Cross? Paula Cholmondeley, CEO of the Sorrel Group, a management consulting company, sits on many boards of directors and knows the corporate world well. When I spoke with her, she advised young people to gain leadership skills in the nonprofit sector. Cholmondeley sees nonprofit organizations such as the National Black MBAs and the National Association

of Black Accountants as offering the kind of leadership opportunities that might not yet be available to young people within
the corporation. Beyond that, being active in the nonprofit sector can provide a tuition-free education. Whether you're interested in the arts, the environment, education, health, or even a
political campaign, working—or volunteering—for an organization dedicated to that cause can give you a chance to shoul-
der responsibility quickly. That's why the experience you gain
at a nonprofit is as useful on a résumé as business experience. If
you receive any recognition for community service, such as an
award, be sure to add it to your résumé.

The next section of your résumé should contain information
about your educational background. If you've gone to college,
there is no need to list your high school. Provide the name of
the institution, your field of specialization, and the degree or
certificate you received. Start out with any educational program you're now attending. In this section I would also include
training; perhaps you've had a two-week seminar in Total
Quality Management or attended two Internet workshops.
Such details could help you stand out.

After your education, list any awards, publication credits,
military experience, and personal information—"married with
two children" for example. If you think the information can
help you, list it.

Many résumé-writing guides advise you to include an
objective—a one-sentence statement that describes your next
career goal. The problem is, this can limit your options. If your
résumé states that your objective is to become a media representative, a department that has an opening for a writer probably wouldn't consider you. To avoid that, you may want to
omit the objective and include instead a succinct, one- or two-
sentence summary of your background and accomplishments.

No résumé is cast in concrete. As you get feedback from potential employers, make appropriate changes. For example, suppose you listed a job as a part-time tarot card reader, and in an
interview you were grilled unpleasantly about it. Maybe you

should leave that off. But if an interviewer gets excited about your work on a reengineering task force, you might want to expand your description of that on your résumé.

Pros—those who earn six figures—usually tailor their résumés for each category of job or each organization. They might have one résumé for jobs in internal communications and another for positions in speechwriting. They may describe their experience differently for a large organization than for a small one. What they are trying to do is make themselves, at least on paper, appear to be an excellent fit for whatever job they might apply for.

So learn from the pros. We all have a variety of experience. Depending on the context, you might want to omit some parts of your experience in a particular résumé and highlight other parts. Be flexible in how you look at your experience. Be prepared to match it to what an organization seems to want.

ATTACHMENTS TO YOUR RÉSUMÉ

When I was young, I was a man in a hurry. For my first job, I was determined to get an offer from a large public relations firm. How did I make this happen? With attachments to my résumé. I sat down and made two lists. One was of the things I could do uniquely well; sure, I had gone to graduate school and could write well, speak well, and drive a car, but so could many other people. It was tough to sort out what I assumed only *I* could accomplish but once I did, my résumé looked stronger. And my confidence soared

The other list focused on what distinguished me from other job candidates. I limited each list to ten items, clipped the two lists to my résumé—and got the job I wanted. The interviewers complimented me on my initiative. I stood out from all the other applicants.

YOUR COVER LETTER

In journalism they call the first paragraph of anything the "grabber." That is, its function is to grab the reader's attention. Your cover letter is your grabber. You want to get the employer's attention. If you don't make a persuasive sales pitch in your cover letter, the employer is unlikely to even look at your résumé.

In the cover letter you highlight the strongest points of your résumé. If you've just completed a cost-reduction program that saved your current company $2 million, put that in. Also put in any other recent major accomplishments. (Leave out less recent accomplishments or those that date back to your school days.) Also include significant leadership posts or accomplishments in nonprofit organizations. What you want the reader to say is, "This applicant really has something to offer and is an excellent fit for the job!"

There are books such as *The Adams Cover Letter Almanac* that can guide your writing. But nothing has greater impact than a letter that is in your own voice and is full of your genuine enthusiasm.

THE STRUCTURE OF THE COVER LETTER

The cover letter should be one page long and have about five sections (or brief paragraphs).

Section one is where you state *why you are writing.* You want to convey enthusiasm about the prospect of working for this organization or in that particular position. For example:

> I'm replying to your ad for a manager of speechwriting at National Widget. I've heard a number of executives from National Widget speak, and I'd like to join the team that produces those terrific speeches.

Another approach might be:

I'm applying for the position of manager of
speechwriting at National Widget. I've followed National
Widget in the business press for a number of years and
would like to be part of such an outstanding organization.

Section two presents your *strongest qualifications for the job.*
Highlight your experience and your accomplishments. You
don't have to rehash everything that is in your résumé, just
what would lead the reader to conclude that you're an excellent fit for the job. For example, your second paragraph might
look like this:

Currently I am director of internal communications
at Global Motors, a recently downsized organization.
In addition to receiving numerous awards for our
newsletters, magazines, and website, we've been a model
for more than fifty downsized organizations on how to
reengineer the internal communications function. Prior
to Global Motors I worked in a public relations agency,
where my team increased profits by 32 percent. I have an
MBA from Harvard Business School and studied in Japan
for two years. I speak fluent Japanese.

The third section contains, if appropriate, any suggestions for
the organization. Here there is a risk, of course. They may already be doing what you suggest or may be offended at the sug-
gestion. However, if you can avoid those two pitfalls, this is a
way to differentiate yourself from the competition. For instance, if you're applying to the promotions department at Mc-
Donald's, you might make suggestions about how to increase
business during the dinner hour.

The fourth section should *demonstrate your knowledge of the organization.* Begin your research with the company's website,
and be sure to learn the names of the CEO and other VIPs, including members of the board. Read the annual report; if it's
not on the website, Google it. Continue your investigation at

DowJones.com, Bloomberg.com, and WSJ.com, the website of the *Wall Street Journal*. In short, do your homework. By becoming thoroughly informed about the organization, you can convincingly explain why you're enthusiastic about joining it. For instance, you could write:

> General Widget's accomplishments in new product development are outstanding. Especially impressive is the Widget System 200. I'd like to be part of the General Widget team.

The fifth section is your request for an interview. That's the action you want the reader to take. So provide phone and e-mail information about how to contact you. Indicate if this application is confidential. And be aware that 37 percent of employers admit to checking out applicants on social media prior to the interview. So make sure your online presence is in keeping with the position you hope to get.

THE INTERVIEW

In the opinion of Roger Ailes—President of Fox News and advisor to US presidents and executives—people form their impressions about you in the first seven seconds of meeting you. That means that when you go for an interview, it's critical how you enter the room, how you make eye contact, and how you shake hands. It's important that you don't sit down until you're invited to do so. Watch the top executives at your organization or the top officials at your college. Notice how they enter a room and make their presence felt.

During the interview, the interviewer might talk more than you do. That's only appropriate. That person will explain the job to you and tell you how the department is structured. However, that doesn't mean you can't speak up and sell yourself. If you notice that the department has a busy pace, briefly describe how you worked effectively in a similar situation. If they're launching a newsletter, briefly tell how you were involved in a similar project. If they just cut the department's budget by 25 percent, explain how you functioned during budget cuts.

You will also be expected to ask questions demonstrating that you have done research on the organization and understand its mission, services, and products. Before you go for the interview, make sure you have a feel for what the organization is all about. Although United Way and the Salvation Army are both nonprofit organizations, they have different orientations.

You may be asked questions about things you'd rather not discuss—such as a job you lost or six months of unemployment. The best way to handle those questions is to be honest about the situation and extremely positive about your response to it. There's no need to be defensive or apologetic. This is your chance to show that you can overcome adversity with your spirit and motivation intact.

This doesn't mean that you have to volunteer information that could be damaging to you. But when you go into an interview, be prepared to discuss the not-so-pleasant aspects of your career. Many organizations have developed ways to find out information about the job candidate—and it's usually *not* by calling your three references. One effective way I've seen job candidates handle negative information is to explain what they've learned from the experience. After all, at this point in your career, you *should* be in a learning mode. Tell the interviewer what you've learned from being fired or out of work for half a year.

After the interview, send a follow-up note to all the key players. Be specific. State what you learned about the organization or job and why that was important to you. Thank them for inviting you. After the interview, if you win an award or write a speech that is quoted in the press, send a note about this to the appropriate people.

NETWORKING

Studies show that most jobs—a full 51 percent—are filled via promotions and transfers within the ranks. The remaining 49 percent are filled in various ways, the most common of which is by referral. The message? It matters whom you know. Networking with other professionals is essential.

The essence of networking, whether online or face-to-face, is attitude. You enter the networking arena with the attitude that you're going to share what you have with others. Networking is a type of bartering. Someone gives you a job lead today; tomorrow, when you're in that job, you'll be in a position to give work or another type of favor to that person. If you don't anticipate that you'll have anything to trade, you don't belong in the network.

When you approach friends and acquaintances, you need to sell them on the idea that you're worth investing in. Therefore, you need to deliver the message that you're highly marketable. This is no place to dwell on your shortcomings.

In approaching potential employers—"sending unsolicited résumés," as it's called—the best procedure is *not* to ask for a job. Instead, ask for ten minutes of the person's time to talk about the company and your career path. Your objective in sending out letters is to get in to see someone. That someone will likely give you the names of other people to see. Here is a sample unsolicited-résumé application:

Mr. Robert Smith
Director of Internal Communications
Global Motors
Detroit, MI 48233

Dear Mr. Smith:
 Congratulations on winning *Business Daily*'s annual new product competition. I would like to learn more about how communications operates at Global Motors.

For five years I've been an information specialist at a consumer products company. We handle everything from the employee newsletter to the annual report. I've learned a tremendous amount through this experience, and my responsibilities have grown accordingly. Last year, I wrote the chairman's letter in the annual report. And this year, I'm solely responsible for all speeches made to employees. But now I'm assessing my career and trying to determine what my next step will be.

Could you perhaps give me ten minutes of your time to discuss Global Motors and my career path? I would be happy to meet you before or after normal business hours, as you prefer.

I'll be calling you next week. Meanwhile, you can e-mail me at _____@_____ or call me at (555) 234-5678. Thank you for your time.

Sincerely,
(your signature, written and typed beneath)

When you do get a good job, don't forget the people who helped or tried to help you. You have a big debt to pay off. Every Christmas, I call forty people who have helped me with my career, even though we may not have talked for a whole year. I fill them in on what's going on in my life and let them know that I remember how they helped me.

Throughout this book I will present interviews with experts in a variety of fields. The first interview is with Jean Allen, a partner in Heidrick & Struggles, an international executive recruiting firm.

INTERVIEW: JEAN ALLEN

RLD: Things have changed since the first edition of this book was published. What's the right way to conduct a job search now?

JA: It's tougher out there, and there's more competition, but some things have remained the same. You still want to create a broad network, and you want to stay very, very positive when you talk to people.

RLD: What's the best way to begin?

JA: Do everything you can to approach people and to offer your credentials. I always tell people this little story: Years ago, I was trying to move a table out of my office on the weekend, and the table got stuck in the doorway. Just as I was thinking that I'd have to climb over it to get out, a woman who was also working on the weekend came along and offered to help. She was another search person. In the course of working together to move that table—it was a lesson in physics!—she told me that she didn't really like being in search. What she wanted to do was internal recruiting inside a company. A couple of days later I got a call from a client looking for an internal recruiting person, and I thought of her immediately. So if you're looking for a job, move a table, which is to say, talk to people. You never know where the right job is going to come from. Also, keep busy—and not just sitting in front of your computer looking at job boards. Do volunteer work. Interact in broad circles not specifically related to your job search, because you'll likely make some meaningful connections. In those ways, the world hasn't changed that much.

RLD: You mentioned job boards. What do you think of them?

JA: The odds are not in your favor on job boards, but they've gotten more sophisticated—and somebody is going to get that job. If you're qualified, your chances are better than they used to be, because only qualified applicants get through.

RLD: Should you approach companies directly?

JA: Yes. Start with a list of companies where you'd like to work. The list can be as long as you want—ten companies, twenty, fifty. Then go to their websites, read everything about the company, and apply.

RLD: What about cover letters?

JA: Now more than ever, it should not be the same cover letter you sent with your last résumé. It should be short, and it should show that you have, for a long time, been interested in this organization, and here's why. If you can catch them in the first couple of lines and show that you really care, that could be just the opening you need.

RLD: Let's talk about résumés.

JA: Keep it simple. What a potential employer wants to see is something that tells a story in a very succinct manner, and the best way to do that is with a traditional résumé: at the top is your most recent position, and then, in reverse chronology, everything else, with your education at the bottom. The only extra is the brief mission statement or summary at the top.

RLD: Should a résumé be on paper or electronic?

JA: Both! People send me electronic résumés, and then, when they show up for a meeting, they bring a paper copy with them. It's gracious and helpful—unless a headhunter sent you in. In that case, you have to assume that they have sent their own version of the résumé, so you don't need to bring one.

RLD: What advice do you have for interviews?

JA: Be very prepared. Be very confident. Be yourself. And have a good sense of what you want to accomplish. Sometimes you've going for a specific job, and sometimes it's just to make a good impression for future refer-

ence. Know what it is you want to get out of that interaction.

RLD: What do you think about informational interviews?

JA: I think they're great. They can be critically important to
somebody looking for a job, and a lot of times that's how
you end up with your job: one thing leads to another.

RLD: What mistakes do job seekers make when they're on the
market?

JA: Sometimes, in the interest of staying focused, they become pests. As a headhunter, I can tell you, there is a
point where job seekers overplay it, and people will
avoid them. Or they feel despairing, and it shows. Or
they get isolated and do everything through their computer. When they're unemployed, they feel they have to
spend their day being productive, so they keep sending
requests for updates. I've been unemployed, so I'm not
saying this from a mountaintop. I understand it. But
sometimes if you get out into the world more, you come
back with more confidence.

RLD: What are the implications of our being in a bad economy?

JA: You have to be even more vigilant about all the things
that you would do in a good market, and you have to be
a very authentic person. There is such a huge flow of information and requests into companies, and they see so
many résumés, but the human aspect hasn't gotten less
important—it's gotten more so.

RLD: I've noticed that, too, and I don't think it's going to
change.

Things to Remember

- In all aspects of the search, customize your pitch to the
  particular organization and job
- Sell yourself through your accomplishments and uniqueness
- Don't be too linear in your job hunt
- Don't get down on yourself if you don't succeed right away

3

ON YOUR OWN

This chapter is must reading IF:

- You want to get beyond the hype about entrepreneurs
- You're thinking about starting a business or buying a franchise
- You wonder if you have the right attitude for self-employment
- You need help starting your business
- And you want to be happy

Have you ever taken one of those quizzes, either online or in a magazine or book, to find out if you should be an entrepreneur? I'll bet you have. When the job situation is difficult, as it has been in recent years, many people think about going out on their own. Perhaps you are one of them. In 2010, according to the US Small Business Administration, entrepreneurs launched approximately 742,000 new businesses. And that's not counting the, literally, millions of people who operate one-person businesses. Even in the midst of a recession, the entrepreneurial spirit asserts itself.

George Gendron, founder and director of the Innovation and Entrepreneurship Program at Clark University and former editor-in-chief of *Inc.,* the magazine of small business, emphasizes that no single personality type makes for a successful entrepreneur. So forget the quizzes. He observes, "Those entrepreneurs who succeed come in all stripes and all sizes and all ages, all personality types, all backgrounds. Some are very conservative. Some take more risks. I think that there are not any consistently identifiable personality traits that successful entrepreneurs have in common."

I agree with Gendron. When I was thinking of starting my business—the Dilenschneider Group—in 1991, I was probably the last person you would have thought would become an entrepreneur. I had a good track record, but it was a track record compiled within organizations. And I wasn't especially hungry; my career in an organization had made me financially comfortable. Nevertheless, I did start my own public relations agency, and it has been successful. That doesn't mean I wasn't scared. I had spent more than twenty years in the corporate cocoon. I had never even had to mail my own letters. But on my very first day as an entrepreneur I immediately became responsible for buying thousands of dollars' worth of office equipment.

Like me, you may be an atypical entrepreneur who winds up becoming successful. And, if you are considering taking the plunge, let me tell you, it's okay to be scared.

In this chapter, it is my intention to free you from all the hype that surrounds entrepreneurship. I'll begin by interviewing Astro Teller, one of the more extraordinary entrepreneurs I know. Dr. Teller is a scientist with degrees in computer science, symbolic computation, and artificial intelligence. Before moving to Google, where he is Director of New Projects, he created several successful businesses, including Cerebellum Capital, a hedge fund, and BodyMedia, a company that makes wearable medical devices that monitor the quality of your sleep, the intensity of your exercise, and the calories you burn. He has even published a couple of novels. So he knows what it means to venture out on his own as an entrepreneur. Here's part of our discussion:

INTERVIEW: ASTRO TELLER

RLD: On your website you describe yourself as an entrepreneur, author, and scientist. I was surprised that you put "entrepreneur" first. What does being an entrepreneur mean to you?

AT: Entrepreneurs are people who thrive on starting new things and have both the bravery to be under-expert at the thing they're going to do and the capacity—the sort of meta-capacity—to become highly capable at the things they'll need to know to make the organization grow.

RLD: Can you give me an example from your own experience?

AT: When I started a hedge fund, I didn't know anything about hedge funds, and I didn't pretend to. What I said to my early investors was, "I have an idea." It was actually a software idea; it just happened that the finance world was an appropriate place for this to play out. I had to ramp up quickly, but I have a track record of figuring out things that I don't know. So I said, "I think your money would be safe with me, or, anyway, it would be a good bet, and I will go learn what I need to learn about the hedge fund world."

RLD: Did you ever think, what have I gotten myself into?

AT: Oh, totally. Every time. Being an entrepreneur is the process of going into an area where you're not an expert and finding, let's say, three rules to break out of the top hundred rules or assumptions of that industry. But you still have to learn the other ninety-seven. Typically what happens is that, when you look at the industry from the outside, you think, how hard can it be? It's only once you're in the industry that you appreciate how incredibly hard it is. That's what happened when I was starting the hedge fund.

RLD: Given the challenges, how should would-be entrepreneurs assess an idea before they commit themselves to it?

AT: People are generally pretty secretive when they try to start businesses, and I think that's foolish. If your idea is so obvious that people are going to steal it if you tell them about it, then you don't have anything special. Whoever wins is going to be the execution king, and usually those are people with more money than you. So you might as well not bother.

I recommend talking to a lot of people—to venture capitalists, to angel investors, to potential lawyers who might help you run the business. I see all that as free consulting. You visit each of these people and tell them what you're thinking. Be honest about what you think the problems and the opportunities are, and get their feedback. You'll learn a lot.

You'll also make ten friends for every one person who's even going to consider stealing your idea. If you go to five lawyers instead of one, and you say, look, I'm starting a project, I want to tell you about my idea, and I want you to give me some feedback on it, you'll get free legal advice, free consulting on your business, and, if you're paying any attention at all, you'll take one new fact or idea out of each meeting. You'll also get a better lawyer than if you just picked one of those five because somebody said that lawyer was good. And it's not just the lawyers; you can do that with the accountants and the venture capitalists and everybody else.

RLD: Many people are intimidated by meeting with venture capitalists.

AT: I enjoy meeting with venture capitalists because I start every meeting by saying, "I don't want your money right now." As soon as I tell them that, it becomes a different meeting. I say, look, I'm going to come back and ask for your money in two years. What I want to do now is just discuss this business with you, and I want you to get to know me. I'm going to come back every six months and give you an update. And by the time we get to two years from now, you're going to see that the business is interesting, the industry is interesting, and I can actually identify meaningful, reasonable milestones and then achieve them. By the time I ask you for money, it's going to be an easy yes. Often they give me money earlier than the two years, but by setting it up that way, they don't feel pressured.

RLD: It also sounds like an effective way to network.

AT: Exactly. I'm networking with them, and they're giving me ideas, whereas if I asked them for money, they would go into critical mode and tell me how bad my idea was. This way, they don't feel that they have to put up their defenses, which is what they typically do as soon as a guy with a goatee and a ponytail walks into their offices. So they can get a little excited, see the positives, brainstorm with me, tell me two people I should talk to.

RLD: You're an outgoing guy. Is that important?

AT: Less than people think. You can be an introvert and still be a great entrepreneur, absolutely.

RLD: What personal qualities do you think an entrepreneur must have?

AT: The most important characteristics are passion, persistence, integrity, and adaptability. If you have those four, it would be hard to lose, and if you're missing one of them, you'd have to get awfully lucky to win. It happens, but it's hard.

Notice that I didn't mention "smart" in that list. I think that having an IQ of 130 is unnecessary, and quite possibly not even useful, in being an entrepreneur, because a lot of entrepreneurship is management and leadership—and, typically, the smarter you are, the harder it is for you to do those things well.

RLD: Why is that?

AT: Smart people believe they can think their way through

these things, when, in fact, what you need is empathy and compassion and experience. That's what it takes to be great at management and leadership. "Smart" doesn't actually help, and sometimes it actively gets in the way.

RLD: What have you found to be the chief satisfactions of being an entrepreneur?

AT: I get a strong sense of personal accomplishment. It feels good to do anything that you're good at, and I like the fact that it pushes me to learn faster than in other environments. When I throw myself into a situation where I am, by many standards, wildly incompetent—such as starting a body-monitoring company when I have no background in health care—it forces me to learn an enormous amount quickly. I like that steep part of the learning curve.

One of the most satisfying jobs of an entrepreneur is to create and nurture an environment, a culture. When you brew a culture that you enjoy being part of, you go to work with excitement. And, of course, that becomes a virtuous cycle. Everyone goes to work with excitement, and everyone works harder, and they feel more like a team, and there's more trust, and they get more work done because they spend less time on office politics. So it works well.

I also feel rewarded when someone in one of my organizations graduates to a higher level of competence. At BodyMedia, we went through a series of secretary/office managers, all of whom were so competent that they graduated, three in a row, to new positions in the organization. Watching their careers flourish, and taking some small credit for the fact that the company was providing them with an opportunity and an environment where they could grow—it made me feel that something even more important than the success or failure of the whole business had happened. I like that feeling.

RLD: What are the greatest challenges to being an entrepreneur?

AT: It can be a lonely and frustrating process. Entrepreneurship involves a lot of ambiguity and risk. Things look great one day and horrible the next and great the day after that, and the emotional challenge—most of it—is finding ways to manage the stress.

RLD: How do you recommend dealing with that?

AT: I think anyone who starts a business without a partner or cofounder does not understand what they're setting themselves up for. I would never start a business by myself. It's an emotional thing, not a practical one. There's something about someone who feels equally responsible with you, someone you don't need to cheerlead, someone you can go out to dinner with and say, "I'm feeling like a failure this evening," and have them pump you back up. Having someone you can turn to is a big deal in my opinion.

RLD: What other mistakes do people make in trying to establish a business?

AT: Oh, they're legion. People raise too little money, they raise too much money, they get addicted to raising money rather than to becoming profitable, they hire people terribly, they don't know how to manage people. Most people do not understand leadership, and they would do a lot better if they spent half their time being empathetic. Being empathetic doesn't mean understanding why the person in the corner is grumpy and then giving him what he wants; it means understanding *everyone* on the team, why they're leaning in different psychological directions, and it means creating an environment and a persona for yourself that's going to work for them as a group. But you can't start without being open to the idea that you're wrong a lot of the time.

          One of my strengths is that, as a manager and a leader,

I actually don't think my ideas are always the best ideas. If you believe that your ideas are the best ideas, then you're stuck with the glass ceiling of your own ideas, and unless you're Steve Jobs, that's a bad deal. I know I'm not Steve Jobs, and I don't think my ideas always need to win over those of others. I often don't even put my ideas on the table, because I don't want them to get in the way. I see my job as creating the nest, and I'm very explicit with my teams that it's their job to lay the eggs. Maybe sometimes I'd rather lay the egg—it's more fun to lay the egg, since no one really gets credit for building the nest—but the weird thing is that, in the end, the CEO gets credit for the egg, anyway. See yourself as a servant to your company, dedicate yourself to building the nest, and make sure that the people in your organization feel empowered to have their own ideas. At the end of the day, if they think that no idea but your idea is going to win, your employees will feel redundant, and they're going to stop doing their job, because they're waiting for you to do it.

RLD: What about hiring people? Do you look for the same traits you described earlier when we were talking about entrepreneurs?

AT: It's basically the same. Of course, sometimes I look for particular expertise because I have a specific role to fill. So if you're a programmer, I need you to know how to program. I'm not going to shy away from verifying that. But that's the easy thing to test for. I'm also looking for passion, persistence, integrity, and adaptability.

RLD: I've heard you say that you only hire people if they have a certain "shining from within." What do you mean by that?

AT: When I sit down with people, I usually know within seconds how intense they are and how present they are. Of course, if you're an intense, passionate, high-integrity person, but you have the flu, you might seem as if you're not really there, and I may pass on you. That's a false negative. I can live with that because I can always interview more people. But it's hard to create a false positive. It's hard to be a good enough actor. People who try can seem manic, but that's not the same as shining.

Often in interviews I will purposely set someone up to be wrong, because the people I really want are the people who will say, "Oh, really? That's cool!" and they move on. They spend no time trying to convince me—or themselves—that they weren't wrong. They're actually interested in knowing what the right answer is. Those people are going to do great.

RLD: How does being an entrepreneur differ from being at a large company like Google?

AT: It's wildly different. If you want to do something that is particularly crazy looking, and you're a stand-alone entrepreneur, just do it—there is no downside. But you can't do that in a large company, because a large company has a valuable brand, which you could meaningfully hurt by doing something that might be seen as irresponsible. Being in a large organization, I face some challenges that I didn't face before and I also have some opportunities I never had. But being an entrepreneur does not always mean that you're out on your own. You can be an entrepreneur within a business. It just means taking responsibility for building something new, and that, I would like to think, is what I do at Google.

RISKS AND BENEFITS

The biggest risk facing entrepreneurs is one that people prefer not to think about: failure. In fact, about 30 percent of new businesses go under within the first two years—and about half fail within five years. That represents a lot of unpaid bills, lost jobs, and dashed dreams. There are no infallible formulas in small business, no guarantee that if you do X, Y, and Z, you'll succeed.

Why do businesses fail? There are any number of reasons. Your business may be feeling the impact of trouble in your industry, of stiff competition, or of poor management. Or it could be a casualty of broad economic trends.

There's no getting around it: Starting a business is a risk. You can fail. Because self-employment has become so popular and so prominent in the media, you might easily forget that no start-up, no small business you buy, and no franchise is ever a sure thing.

But as a generation you're well positioned to take the risk of starting a business. For us in the Silent Generation and for the Baby Boomers, there was plenty of motivation to go to a big organization, stay there for our entire career, and ultimately enjoy the pension that came with medical benefits. That option no longer exists for you. Jeff Porten, who is a member of Generation X, started an international consulting firm specializing in new media technologies and the Internet. Porten wrote a book about his journey to self-employment called *The Twentysomething Guide to Creative Self-Employment: Making Money While Keeping Your Freedom.*

On the very first page Porten says that his generation is the "first generation in the history of our culture in which most people think their own lives will not be better than their parents' lives." He goes on to say that the volatile global economy and the lack of good jobs have left many of you in a "constant state of low-level fear, uncertainty, and doubt." For Porten the ticket out of that situation was starting his own business.

For you, the upside of self-employment could be tremendous opportunity at a relatively low "opportunity cost." The upside could be a living wage—plus the freedom to decide how you will live and work. You might even become rich. As for "opportunity costs," they will probably be minimal for you.

What are "opportunity costs"? They are the returns or revenues you would have received if you had *not* started a business but instead worked for a GE or an IBM during that time. For instance, let's say you're working full-time for GE and earning a respectable salary plus benefits. That might be difficult for you to trade in for zero compensation as an entrepreneur. For most of my career, the opportunity cost of starting my own business was very high. In those days salaries were excellent. And that opportunity cost deterred many employees who really wanted to start a business.

That, of course, is not your situation. Your opportunity cost probably isn't significant. You might only be risking a low salary when you decide to start your own business. Also, because of your youth, you have the stamina to put in the eighteen-hour days starting a business will require. You have the education to do your own market research and then interpret your findings. And you have the imagination to bootstrap it. That's because you're comfortable thinking on a what-if level. Also, you have a healthy disregard for doing things the conventional way.

THE ENTREPRENEURIAL MIND-SET

How can you know you're doing the right thing in starting a business? You can never be 100 percent certain, especially if you're walking away from a good job with a healthy salary and benefits. Whether the economy is rocky or rock-solid, starting a business means living with insecurity, doubt, and the occasional unwelcome surprise. Only you know whether you have the fortitude to handle that.

Karin Abarbanel is a writer and entrepreneur who understands these issues. In *Birthing the Elephant: The Woman's Go-For-It! Guide to Overcoming the Big Challenges of Launching a Business,* written with Bruce Freeman, she states—and I heartily agree—that "In making this move, you're not just changing your job, or changing your lifestyle, or changing careers, you are changing your identity." It's not merely exchanging one gray hat for a newer gray hat. It's opting for a whole new type of hat—or maybe no hat at all.

All of a sudden, for example, you go from being the person giving vendors work to being the vendor asking for work. It's a humbling experience. The world stops treating you with deference, and you can no longer identify yourself socially as part of a brand-name organization such as GE or Nabisco. Until your business gets off the ground, your professional identity is in limbo. And unlike the office—where, despite downsizing, bonding still exists—it can get pretty lonely out there on your own. That massive identity shift took me by surprise. At the time, though, I wanted my own shop enough to get me past the disorientation.

You, too, can get through the transition if you enter self-employment with the right mind-set.

According to Abarbanel, that mind-set has four major components.

1. **A strong commitment to the business you choose.** You don't just decide to sell cupcakes because it's a hot fad. By the time you get your business launched, the fad will probably be over. You can guarantee staying power for yourself, through thick and thin, only if you love the business you choose. I love public relations.
2. **The willingness to invest enormous amounts of time.** The oldest entrepreneurial joke is that the entrepreneur trades in forty hours a week to work eighty hours. There's just no shortcut around that time demand. Can your family life withstand this pressure?
3. **A strong desire to operate independently.** Independence is the heartbeat of entrepreneurship. If you're most comfortable working in someone else's organization, you probably don't want to be an entrepreneur. Your freedom has to be more important to you than a regular paycheck.
4. **A realistic, clear-eyed view of the demands involved.** One of the demands in many businesses is the ability to sell a product or a service. If you've never sold before, take a part-time sales job and see if you can sur-

vive out there. In your own business you'll probably also have to do a lot of paperwork, keep the books, and make tough decisions about hiring, about firing, about whether to retain an unprofitable client. As an entrepreneur, you'll have a very diverse job description.

To Abarbanel's four imperatives I would add:

An emotional support system. Maybe it's your family or friends. Maybe it's your former colleagues. You need them not only to encourage you but also to tell you the truth. When I was starting my own shop, I had tremendous support. I went to visit my friend Jack Malloy at DuPont. I was riding high. Malloy asked me, "Bob, you've been blessed with a lot of support, but who's supporting your wife?" I got right up from the chair and called my wife back in New York. I apologized to Jan for not supporting her. It was pretty emotional.

HELP FOR THE ENTREPRENEUR

If you do decide to go into business for yourself, there's great flexibility in how you structure your business. You can become a sole proprietor, create a general or limited partnership, or incorporate yourself. As your business changes, you can change its structure. Before you make a decision about the structure of your business, you should read about the advantages and disadvantages of each. Books such as *Start Your Own Business: The Only Start-Up Book You'll Ever Need,* published by the Entrepreneur Press, are helpful. Nonetheless, you may also have to pay for the expertise of a tax expert and a lawyer. It's the cost of doing business.

The good news is that there's a lot of help out there. Besides networking with other entrepreneurs, which is always a smart thing to do, you will find a variety of other resources.

THE SMALL BUSINESS ADMINISTRATION

The US Small Business Administration (SBA) is the first place to go for information. The website (SBA.gov) is extensive and detailed. Plus, if you have questions—and you will—you can contact someone there directly, either via e-mail (answerdesk@sba.gov) or by phone (800-827-5722). The SBA fields calls from entrepreneurs in all phases of business. They may be starting out. They may need free counseling or training or disaster assistance. They might want to go public. The first stop for all those issues can be the SBA, which, besides the main office in Washington, DC, has 10 regional offices, 69 state offices, 110 Women's Business Centers, and about 900 Small Business Development Centers across the country. It's a major resource.

SCORE—the Service Corps of Retired Executives—works closely with the SBA to provide advice and mentoring free of charge.

The SBIC—the Small Business Investment Corporation—makes funds available and offers management expertise.

OTHER FEDERAL AGENCIES

There are many resources for entrepreneurs within the federal government. In addition to the SBA, you can learn a lot at business.USA.gov, an online clearinghouse for small businesses. The site also offers a list of other government organizations that provide specialized assistance, such as the Department of Veterans Affairs, the US Patent and Trademark Office, the Minority Business Development Agency, and many more.

Help from Uncle Sam may be especially useful if you're considering an import or export business. For example, if you are interested in exporting food, there are the Foreign Agriculture Service (FAS), the FAS Trade Assistance and Promotion Office, the FAS Trade Show Office, and the Department of Agriculture's Farmers Market Promotion Program.

THE PUBLIC LIBRARY AND THE BOOKSTORE

The Internet is a great and wonderful thing, but it would be a mistake to do your research only there. If your local library is oriented toward business, you will discover that a reference librarian can assist you with market research and alert you to resources you might never have unearthed on your own.

Browsing in a brick-and-mortar bookstore, if you're lucky enough to have one nearby, can be inspiring. Not only can you find books there that delve into every aspect of business, you will see a surprising number devoted to specific enterprises. Recently, browsing in a Barnes & Noble near my office, I noted books on starting a craft business, a consulting business, a restaurant, a coffee bar, a bed-and-breakfast, a wedding-planning business, even a nonprofit. And don't forget to look at business magazines. *Forbes, Fortune, Fast Company, Inc., The Economist* and other periodicals will keep you current.

HANG IN THERE

If this veteran entrepreneur could give the new entrepreneur one gift, that gift would be persistence. Look at John Grisham, whose legal thrillers have sold hundreds of millions of copies. When he was starting out as a novelist, he got up at 5:00 AM to write before going to his day job as a lawyer. After three years, he began sending his manuscript to agents and publishers. *A Time to Kill* was rejected again and again—dozens of times—before a small publisher took a chance on an unknown writer and published it. It received little notice. But he was dogged. He kept writing. It was his second book, *The Firm,* that launched his career. Persistence is more important than imagination, capital, and even luck.

Things to Remember

- There is no one personality type that characterizes successful entrepreneurs
- Your business can fail
- When considering self-employment, calculate the opportunity cost
- There's plenty of help out there, including other entrepreneurs and federal agencies

4

YOU AND YOUR BOSSES

This chapter is must reading IF:

- You're having trouble with the boss
- You have a new boss
- There's an in-crowd in your office, and you're not in it
- You realize that the boss has tremendous power over you

Most people don't like working with bosses. It's not part of human nature to be "bossed around." Go into any ladies' room, any men's room, or any cafeteria in a commercial building, and—if the bosses aren't there—you'll usually get an earful about someone's boss.

Industry Week conducted a survey about bosses; less than 40 percent of the respondents thought that their bosses had adequate managerial and personal skills. Columbia University psychologist Harvey Hornstein conducted an eight-year study of abuse by bosses; he found that 90 percent of the American workforce has, at some time, been subject to abusive behavior from a boss. The resulting stress can seep into every corner of life. A ten-year Swedish study tracking 3,122 men showed that those with incompetent bosses had significantly more heart attacks than those who worked for reasonable people. Numerous other studies from around the world have confirmed that finding: Bad bosses are dangerous to your health.

A BOSS IS A BOSS IS A BOSS . . .

If you think your bosses cause you problems, you're not alone. I've had plenty of tough bosses. In fact, I've worked for seven of the ten bosses once rated by *Fortune* as the toughest in America. After I got to know them, though, they all turned out to be decent human beings.

In most cases, bosses are just human beings under a great deal of pressure. I've never had a "bad"—or evil—boss, per se.

In the army, for example, I was an eager beaver. After I finished what I was supposed to be doing, I went to Corporal Nidel and asked, "What can I do now?" The corporal was having none of that. He told me to move all the rocks from one side of a road to the other side. When I finished that, I again asked what I could do. He told me to move the rocks back to their original position. Was Corporal Nidel a sadist? A bad boss? A power-monger? Not at all. The corporal was simply a boss with a message to deliver. And that message was, "Leave me alone, kid." I got the message.

Some bosses have been downright kind to me. In a public relations agency where I worked, I was supervised at one period by John O'Connell. O'Connell wrote up a strategy for positioning a client. I read it. I did some thinking. And I told O'Connell that his work "needed to be beefed up." The boss invited me to try my hand at the project. I sat at my typewriter—all we had were trusty Selectrics in those days—for hours, without writing a word. Finally I put something down. I gave it to O'Connell. He thanked me very much. However, he thought it "too sophisticated" for this client, he said. He was going to save it for another type of client. Years later I realized the material I'd given him was terrible. I'm glad I had some bosses who allowed me to learn things on my own.

SUCCESSFUL EMPLOYEES

Successful people, I've found, don't waste their time bad-mouthing their bosses. There's no benefit in that—and the boss may find out about what you're saying. (There are "moles" in almost every organization. See Chapter 5.) Successful people accept the fact that bosses are a reality in their lives. They don't expect the boss to change. They understand that if they obtain too much power, the boss might not be pleased. So they maneuver themselves away from a power struggle with the boss. They recognize that the boss may have a lot of responsibility but too little actual authority in the firm, and they're helpful with this situation. They're not afraid of the boss and know how to express their concerns diplomatically. They realize that some bosses just want to hang on until retirement, and they refrain from trying to force new perspectives on the boss. In short, successful people excel in the art of managing their bosses. There's no boss they can't manage.

UNSUCCESSFUL EMPLOYEES

Colleagues of mine, such as Gary S., who didn't accept the reality regarding bosses, ended up with damn-with-faint-praise recommendations, embarrassing raises, and more stress than the rest of us faced. In addition, such employees are generally the first ones let go in a layoff.

Another colleague, Beth R., thought she could ignore the bosses and just work around them. Bad idea. During her performance review, she was labeled "unmanageable" and put on probation.

EMPOWERMENT AND ALL THAT

You might be thinking: "Yeah, that's how bosses were in your day, Bob, but things have changed."

Have they?

Yes, we're hearing a lot about "empowerment" and "leaderless" teams and a "nonhierarchical workplace." But bosses aren't going away. That's because of the laws of accountability. *Somebody* has to be in charge. It's human nature to look to someone for leadership. When I obtain a new client, the first question I ask about the firm is: "Who's in charge?" When I meet the person or persons in charge, *then* I know how to handle the account—because they have the power. Today, bosses may no longer act as if they're the ones in charge, but the change is in the *style* of management. The change is not in the *concept* of power. Even though you might call your bosses "coaches" instead of bosses, they still have awesome power over you. They can fire you. They can promote you. They can make your life miserable.

Companies now hire human resources experts to help traditional bosses act more like coaches or facilitators rather than the deities they used to be. But don't kid yourself. No matter how they appear or act, no matter how nonhierarchical or easygoing they may seem to be, no matter how much they praise you for your input, bosses are bosses are bosses.

MANAGING THE BOSS—A MUST

In this chapter, let's look at why bosses act the way they do—including driving us up the wall. And then let's see how you can bring these people under control—and make your own life easier—by learning to manage them. This is not a new idea. Indeed, it has become something of a contemporary cliché to say that you have to manage the boss. I would go further. I'm convinced you're putting yourself at serious risk if you don't manage your boss. Just like a marketing program, a budget, or the recall of a product, bosses must be managed. If they're not managed properly, someone usually gets smashed—and more often than not it's the employee. You owe it to your career to start thinking about bosses strategically.

PERCEPTION

Often bosses we label "bad" aren't really *that* bad. We just perceive them as "that bad." It's only in hindsight that I have recognized some of my former bosses' strengths and realized that they weren't out to derail my career. In fact, I seldom even came up on their radar screen. I wasn't that important. They had bigger game to bag.

I've investigated why underlings frequently see the boss in a negative light, even when the boss is, in fact, okay. I've talked to employees. I've run online searches. I've read. I've talked to bosses.

One reason we may resent bosses is that we want to *be* the boss. The longing to be Number One is probably what got Satan kicked out of heaven and banished to hell. Satan, like so many of us, didn't like having a boss.

Second, the bosses' power over us is usually immense—so immense that we become obsessed with them. As a result, as with any distortion, the way we see them is often not accurate. A mere jerk becomes a monster in our minds. A lazy boss becomes an evil entity who cruelly piles work on us. We ascribe all kinds of dark motives to bosses who are merely inept.

Third, this is an age of economic angst. Between December 2007 and February 2010, 8.4 million jobs were lost in America. Since then, the situation has improved, but now we all know how easy it is to lose a job. Ours could be next. And bosses have a say in whether we stay or go. It may be in our personal, emotional self-interest to demonize them, but it is not in our interest professionally. Difficult though it may be, we need to rein in our reactions and keep cool.

REALITIES

Of course, many bosses do have problems and can cause us problems. In *Problem Bosses,* Mardy Grothe and Peter Wylie point to eight reasons why:

1. Bosses are ordinary people.
2. Being a boss is a tough job.
3. Bosses often had poor role models.
4. Bosses usually don't become bosses because of their ability to manage people.
5. Bosses often don't get good training.
6. Bosses aren't necessarily expert at handling power and authority.
7. Bosses aren't always held accountable by *their* bosses.
8. Bosses seldom get the feedback they need from employees.

What Grothe and Wylie are saying is that the person who does our performance review and determines our raises is an ordinary human being. Thus, we should have no greater expectation of that boss than we do of any other person in our life. When you think "boss," think "ordinary"; you'll save yourself some disappointment. Those bosses who are truly great leaders are rare—and even they are capable of throwing temper tantrums once in a while.

Being the boss has always been tough. That's because bosses are often "sandwiched" between a rock and a hard place. Above them are *their* bosses, who can hammer away at them. Below them are subordinates, some of whom are crybabies. Now, in a downsized universe, it's even tougher. Bosses must do more with less. On top of all that, they can no longer act like omnipotent autocrats and chew you out for not doing enough. That must be frustrating for them.

Jeff Olson, former editor of *Soundview Executive Book Summaries,* has observed that the best-selling executive business books are those in which the bosses credit their employees—not themselves—for their achievements. We've all read books and articles—or listened to podcasts—about how bosses ought to behave. When we go into work, we expect our bosses to be just like those theoretical bosses. But when you use such idealistic models, you're bound to be disillusioned.

Today's bosses face a big question: How should they behave at work?

For their own role models, bosses often had only their own bosses, whose top-down approaches may be incompatible with today's more diverse, egalitarian workplace.

Frequently, too, bosses have no special gift for managing people or projects. Often they have risen through the ranks because they were good at performing a certain task—such as selling or writing speeches—yet managing projects and people is what they get promoted to do. Often this is like being shipped to France to run an office when you don't know a word of the language. Not surprisingly, bosses face tremendous stress in their managerial activities. Many even *know* they're doing about a B-minus job.

Many organizations don't train their bosses to be bosses. Most bosses don't even know what an appropriate leadership mindset should be. As a result, they're often preoccupied with themselves and their troubles on the job rather than being 100 percent focused on you, the troops.

And, as they say, it can be lonely at the top. If bosses are unused to handling power and authority, there aren't too many people they can buttonhole to discuss the problem.

Many organizations say that their people are their most important asset. Still, bosses are not likely to lose their jobs because they handle subordinates badly. That's yet another reason that they're likely to make mistakes supervising you. Who's going to blow the whistle on them? And, even if someone does, who will care? Few in management will, so long as the shabby treatment doesn't generate any lawsuits.

Up until a few years ago, bosses didn't receive feedback from the troops. That's changing. The advent of "360-degree feedback" is making bosses aware of their impact on subordinates as well as on their superiors. This may or may not improve conditions for employees. The benefits 360-degree feedback can bring depend primarily on how the instrument is used. So don't hold your breath waiting for your bosses to have a spiritual awakening and start treating you much, much better. And if you're asked to participate in a 360-degree evaluation, keep your comments generic. Although those who administer the process claim to maintain strict confidentiality, if you have a concern that is specifically yours—such as the firm's lack of family-friendly policies—your bosses may be able to figure out who criticized them for being inflexible.

To Grothe and Wylie's eight reasons why bosses can be a problem, I would like to add a few of my own.

It's easy for bosses to experience role confusion—and, thus, in turn, confuse us—because they have the capacity to both punish and reward. They represent both the carrot and the stick, the good cop and the bad. I don't know of too many ordinary human beings who can be comfortable with that ambiguity. Bosses need our compassion. They're dealing with a new universe, often without a map.

In addition, bosses sometimes don't make much more money than some of their staff do. They know the staff's salaries and bonuses. When the numbers are close to their own, there is little incentive for them to pull out the stops and do a dynamite job. In that situation, bosses sometimes don't strive for excellence—and that can irk us. After all, many of us assume that our performance is continuously excellent, and we want the boss to be as virtuous as we are. But is our performance *always* that good?

WHO WAS THAT MASKED MAN—OR WOMAN?

I'm convinced that your only option in the workplace is to manage your boss. Any other strategy can have dangerous side effects—such as getting fired.

The secret to managing your bosses—or managing up, as it is sometimes called — is to find out who they are. I mean this broadly. You need to know:

What are the external and internal pressures on them? Are their bosses hammering them to meet an impossible deadline? Did their teenage child just get arrested for using drugs? Have they hit sixty years of age and worry that they will be forced to retire? Let's think of the bosses in human terms rather than as enemies. In managing the boss, you *humanize* rather than *demonize*.
What are the boss's goals? Does your boss want to become CEO or just increase market share 5 percent? Usually bosses have multiple goals. Try to come up with five goals you think your boss might have.
What are the boss's strengths and weaknesses? We all have them. Indeed, usually our weaknesses outnumber our strengths. When you do a strengths/weaknesses "audit" of the boss, be prepared for the weaknesses column to exceed the strengths. Once I got savvy about the world of bosses, I considered it a major strength that the executive simply was breathing. The higher you put your standards for how bosses *should* act, the harder you're going to fall when a particular boss doesn't measure up. Remember breathing—it's a major strength.
What is his or her career history? Is your boss on the defensive these days or on a roll? We have become the people we are today in good measure because of our past. What do you know about your boss's past? In particular, you need to know what setbacks he or she may have faced. How did your boss handle adversity?
     Anyone who has decision-making power today is bound to suffer a setback from time to time. You simply can't do things and not have some of them turn out wrong. Some professions, such as financial services, leave you with more setbacks than others. But a setback can be a transforming experience—so you'd better know that about your boss.
How does your boss work? That style of work should become *your* style. Some bosses read the *Wall Street*

Journal on their commute in and expect that you have
also read it before *you* come into work. You irritate them
when you sit at your desk, on company time, poring over
the day's newspapers. At US Gypsum, when Gene Miller
was the chief financial officer, he would let important
information drop while you were standing at a coffee bar
or boarding a plane. You had to be alert to catch what he
was saying whenever he was saying it. At Bendix, former
chief executive officer Bill Agee liked to hold meetings
over milk and cookies.

How are your bosses changing? Did one just get a
promotion? Is another going through a divorce? All of
this can affect the dynamics between you.

MUTUAL DEPENDENCE

Why is it so important that you know who your bosses really
are and how they work? You and your boss are in a relationship marked by mutual dependency. Neither of you can get by
without the other. Yet some employees find it difficult to acknowledge that reality. They seem unaware that their actions,
attitudes, and decisions can have an enormous impact on the
boss, for good or for ill. I'll bet we all know of bosses who got
sandbagged by the troops and were forced out of the organization. Yes, bosses have tremendous power over you, but you also
have tremendous power over them. Bad-mouthing bosses on
the grapevine is one way you can do them in—but be aware of
unintended consequences.

DIGGING FOR INFORMATION

ABOUT THE BOSSES

When you have new bosses, your number one job is to find
out who these people are, what the pressures on them are, and
how they work. The place to begin is the company plan and

any other information—internal or external—that states the company's goals, where the company is, and where it wants to go. All this is shaping your bosses' mind-set, moods, and goals. You can usually obtain internal information simply by asking for it. I would start by asking the bosses themselves. External information is available online. You can also ask your broker about the company. Read the daily and weekly trade press to keep up with how the company is doing.

The next step is to take the time to learn about your boss in one-to-one meetings. There's no substitute for this. You get to see their body language as well as listen to their words. Admittedly, it's tough to get bosses to give you face time, but it's not impossible. At McDonald's, Dick Starman of the public affairs department was having a difficult time getting in to talk with the CEO. Then he had an idea. He booked the seat right next to his boss on a flight to Tokyo. He even paid for his own first-class ticket. That gave Starman twelve hours to find out what the CEO needed from him.

It's up to you to find out where and when the bosses might be up for a conversation with you. It may be before meetings—so get there early. It may be during a sports activity or when they're doing their volunteer work for United Way. Can you be there, also? Anyone who whines to me that the bosses are "too busy to see me" hasn't used sufficient initiative and imagination.

Another way to find out about the bosses is to ask around. Here, though, you risk word of your questions getting back to them. Often it's easy to get this type of information without consequences if you casually ask the biggest talkers in the organization about the bosses. Just don't be too intense about it.

Be alert for patterns. We all have them, and so do your bosses. Do they prefer to discuss business in formal meetings and engage in small talk only outside meetings? Do they like brief summaries or highly detailed ones? Do they like to see you at your desk after 5:00 P.M.? Those are the things you need to know if you are going to work effectively and efficiently with them. Write down all the bosses' patterns. Conceptualize how you can be a better fit in their world. For example, if the bosses like short reports, how can you eliminate wordiness?

You can also get a good feel for your bosses by listening carefully to their war stories. If you hear a number of stories about how they and the team were in the office until 9:00 P.M. on Christmas Eve, it's pretty obvious they believe in a strong work ethic. These war stories deliver a clear message: *This is what I value.*

And nothing changes a situation like change. You've got to monitor your bosses to keep up to date with what's happening in their lives. One change, such as taking on a huge mortgage, can change everything. Under such circumstances your boss might become more cautious—or even downright risk-averse—seemingly overnight.

The prerequisite for really knowing your boss is empathy. In his breakthrough book *Emotional Intelligence,* Daniel Goleman describes empathy as the capacity to read the emotions of others and know how they feel. That can entail interpreting everything from their gestures to the tone of their voices to their facial expressions. Our capacity for empathy builds on our own self-knowledge. The better we can read or decode our own feelings, the deeper will be our capacity for empathy. And empathy is the key to success in any organization.

ABOUT YOURSELF

In order to be a true help to your bosses, you must also know yourself. For example, your strength in writing could compensate for your bosses' weakness in that area. Maybe you're brilliant at reading the political winds, and your boss isn't. You can help out. And if your bosses belong to the Silent or the Baby Boom Generation, they almost certainly know nothing about social media. You can be their point person.

On the other hand, perhaps your biggest fear is losing a loved one, and your boss lost her husband two years ago. That could make you feel hostile or anxious for all the wrong reasons. Know who you are and what you're feeling.

Also, be clear about your goals and values. Maybe the boss wants to make you a double agent in the department, surreptitiously spying on and reporting about your colleagues, and your values won't let you take on that role. People who know themselves rarely get into ethical hot water.

Self-knowledge shouldn't be any great mystery to you. Start out with a list of the ten things that mean the most to you. And I mean ten, not eleven. That should capture exactly who you are. You might notice that interesting work is more important to you than money. Maybe spending time with your family is more important to you than slaving overtime for a promotion. Or perhaps you find out that you're more ambitious than you thought you were.

Next, make two more lists: your strengths and your weaknesses. Your weaknesses will no longer hurt you if you're aware of and able to compensate for them. Remember, like your boss's, your weaknesses column will probably be longer than your strengths column. Centuries ago, Shakespeare reminded us that we, even the kings among us, are highly flawed human beings. Often, what makes us successful is understanding, taming, and controlling our weaknesses rather than dazzling folks with our strengths.

To make sure you're not deluding yourself, ask a good friend to check out your three lists to see if they're accurate.

A MATCH

Every day when you go into work, you want to determine—quickly—where there is a match between your bosses' goals, strengths, and weaknesses and yours. If the bosses are pros in marketing, and so are you, that's a match. If the bosses are weak in computers, and you're a whiz, that's also a match—because it means you can help them out. They need you. The more matches there are, the better your relationships with the bosses will be.

Matches are what count. I've seen very ordinary employees

get big promotions simply because they made it their business to be helpful to their bosses. People who make it into the bosses' inner circles are people who help the bosses.

THE "RIGHT BOSS"

There is this mythical entity called the "right boss." Well, despite all the talk about it, the "right boss" doesn't exist. *You're* the one who makes the fit with the boss "right." I've never had a boss I couldn't create matches with. Maybe I didn't like the boss. Maybe he had a temper. Maybe he sometimes underestimated me. But, boy, could we work together. As a result, I became a "pet" in the department rather than a "pig." The pigs—those who were oblivious to the bosses' needs—were always the first to be blamed for a problem, the first to be laid off, and the last to get perks such as specialized training that could lead to raises or promotions.

BEWARE OF CHANGES

But situations change. Perhaps the great fit you once had with your bosses has become a little less great. Instead of focusing on increased market share—an arena in which you excel— they've turned to cost reduction, an arena in which you're clueless. You have a number of options.

You can get up to speed on cost reduction. Ask the bosses whom you should talk with. Do an online search on cost reduction. Go to the library and take out some books on the topic. Are there courses at the local college on reducing costs? Do organizations such as the Wharton Business School offer seminars? Let your bosses know you are trying to retool. But don't neglect your usual work.

You can also slowly and carefully search for another job within the company or outside. If your bosses find out about your job hunt, have a response prepared. One valid response would be that the new orientation of the department doesn't utilize your strengths.

If you have been a quick study in other areas that were new

to you, you can be a quick study in this, too. Your best sources of information are other people. Concentrate on learning the language of this field. Don't blab about how new and alien all this is to you. Bosses don't want to hear about anyone's insecurities. You want to show up for the game ready to play.

WHEN THE BOSS IS FOREIGN

In twenty-first century America, you might find that your boss hales from overseas. I've had bosses with roots in every part of the globe. What I always did was learn about each boss's culture. If the boss was Polish, I'd get together with some Polish friends to talk about what made that culture tick. Before going to Australia on business, I'd read the history of that country. I'd also take the time to learn about the country's customs. After all, I was going to be a guest in their land. When the country I was visiting used a language other than English, I made sure I knew the basics, starting with "thank you." That showed my host that I was at least trying.

Ultimately, working well with "foreign" bosses is no different than working with bosses from your own ethnic group. You have to find out what they want to achieve, what their strengths and weaknesses are, and what their work patterns are. Employees who have big problems with bosses from other cultures probably never took the time to learn about those cultures.

Things to Remember

- The boss is the boss
- You can—and must—manage your boss
- Humanize, don't demonize, your boss
- Help the boss out
- There is no one "right" boss for you

5

WORKING THE GRAPEVINE

This chapter is must reading IF:

- There's a rumor on the grapevine about you, and you don't know what to do about it
- People seem guarded when you ask questions on the grapevine
- You get plenty of information on the grapevine, but you wonder if all this isn't a little sleazy

Twenty-one percent of those surveyed about their organization's grapevine admitted they "frequently participated." *Twenty-one percent*—that should be more like 98 percent! With all the volatility and uncertainty in professional life, I don't know anyone who *doesn't* work the office grapevine these days. That's true in large organizations and smaller ones. The grapevine has always been around, but, thanks to the power of technology and social media, it is more important now than it has ever been. Ignore it at your peril.

THE GRAPEVINE = SURVIVAL

The grapevine operates face-to-face, over the telephone, through e-mail, texting, and social media, and, yes, the old-fashioned way—at the water cooler. At one time, you could choose to ignore it. You could sit at your desk and be oblivious to the breaking news of office politics. No more. Now your survival in the workplace—as well as in your own business—depends on how well you're able to work the grapevine.

In this chapter you'll learn what the grapevine consists of, how you can get information from it, how you can plant information in it, and how to "turn around" rumors about yourself or a friend. You'll also find out that, contrary to popular belief about the grapevine, it does have a conscience.

THE POWDER BLUE SUIT

The power of the grapevine first became clear to me when I was working at the Chicago office of a public relations firm and living in Wilmette, Illinois. My wife and I had given a dinner party—one we thought was quite successful. But the talk on the commuter train the next morning was not about the success of the party. It was about one of the guests. He had worn a powder blue suit, when the rest of us were wearing dark ones. By 9:00 AM, just about every professional working in Chicago knew about the suit caper. That man's ability to conduct business in the Chicago area was finished. Could he have recovered from this? You bet. But either he didn't know how, or he didn't ask anyone's help. And he faded from the scene. After that, I clearly saw that the grapevine was not just a rumor mill. It helped to determine who was fit to do business in town. Like God, it made judgments.

THIS THING CALLED "THE GRAPEVINE"

In *Corporate Cultures,* Terrence Deal and Allan Kennedy call the grapevine a company's "cultural network." This network is the primary means of communication within an organization, and, unlike all the other functions in that organization, it operates without regard to rank or status. The grapevine is a democratic institution. Those with access to power—and, therefore, information—can have a lot more clout than you might expect on the grapevine. They include administrative assistants, secretaries, and executive assistants. To get in, all you need is for them to like—and trust—you.

The grapevine works quickly. Twenty years ago, Keith Davis studied the grapevine in a manufacturing company. At eleven o'clock one evening, a manager's wife had a baby. By two the next afternoon, 46 percent of the company's employees knew about the birth. True, by today's standards, that sounds laughably slow. On the Internet, the grapevine operates at warp speed. News—or rumors—can spread in a flash. And, if you're not careful, that flash can cause permanent harm to your reputation.

Messages travel the grapevine in the form of "headlines." Gordon Allport, the well-known psychologist, wrote in *The Psychology of Rumor:* "As a rumor travels, it tends to grow shorter, more concise, more easily grasped and told." A message may start out as "Kramer unfairly fired by headquarters." But soon it will travel as "Kramer canned."

STARTING OUT

If you're alert, likeable, and willing to invest some time, you can learn to work any grapevine in any organization. There are professionals, such as media relations person Richard Kosmicki, who are geniuses at connecting with the right people and gaining their trust. As a result, Kosmicki has an excellent track record of pairing up the right reporter at the right publication or television show with his client at just the right time. All this goes back to Kosmicki's days as a newspaper reporter, when he learned to tap the right sources for his stories.

Maybe you won't become a Kosmicki, but you can do well enough on the grapevine to protect your job and advance your career. You may be new at your job or at running a business. Let's see how you can access the grapevines you need.

NEW AT WORK

Being new at something is a little overwhelming. You may want to hide during those first few weeks. Bad move.

If people at your organization are going to pass along information to you, they have to know you. (They also have to know you can be trusted to "protect your sources"—that is, not reveal the name of the person who gave you the information.) Therefore, you should be accessible. If coworkers come to your door, stop what you're doing, stand up, and talk to them. If you have the time, invite them to take a seat. Or make a lunch appointment. But this shouldn't be your only entrée to the grapevine. Search out *sub*-grapevines, those that feed into material outside of the main grapevine. Maybe this sub-grapevine is the weekly Weight Watchers meeting at the company. Maybe it's all those employees with preteens at the Country Day School. Or it could be everyone who's going to school at night. Because people in such groups come from all parts of the organization, they can become founts of information.

You should also connect with grapevines in other departments, not just your own. Suppose you do business with the finance department. After a while, if they get to know you, they'll share information with you about what's going on there. Another type of grapevine might be social circles you don't normally travel in. Make an effort to be friends with people at work who are *not* the kind of people you would normally socialize with. Invite them to lunch or to golf on Saturday. If you restrict yourself to people just like yourself, you'll wind up restricting the kind of information you gain access to.

It pays to be tolerant on a grapevine. We normally make

judgments about others, but doing so openly could work against you on the grapevine. Suppose you take an instant dislike to Peter Jones from the mailroom because he talks too much. Well, Jones may be an excellent source of information. Someday Jones may be your champion and tell everybody about the long hours you put in. There's simply no value in being critical of people on the grapevine. There's also the principle of reciprocity. If you openly dislike someone, that person is bound to dislike you, and then you lose a contact on the grapevine.

SELF-EMPLOYMENT

Working for yourself doesn't free you from needing to seek out information on the grapevine. If fact, because you're more or less alone out there, you need information *more* than an employee in a large company does. And you need it from all sorts of grapevines. You will need to penetrate the grapevine at all your clients' shops. You will need to find out what's really going on throughout your industry. And you will need to know what other entrepreneurs in the community are doing. Are those entrepreneurs as slow in getting orders as you, or are you doing something wrong in your business? Then there are the suppliers in your industry. Because they live or die based on the orders they receive, they usually have a good feel for what's happening.

Since you are simultaneously marketing your services and asking for orders, you usually have less power than your client. Therefore, when you go to the client's organization, you have to be careful how you penetrate the grapevine there. Some clients like to keep vendors on a short leash and don't want you talking to others in the organization. If so, you'll have to respect that. Never wander around an organization unless you know your client would approve of it. In many client–vendor relationships, the grapevine turns out to be one person: your client. And that client is not likely to share information with you if you pose too many questions too intensely.

Another way to penetrate the grapevines of client organizations, supplier groups, and entrepreneurs is to join the professional associations those people belong to. You may come away with not only information but also new business.

I've found that the dumbest mistake self-employed people can make is to assume they are *part* of the clients' organizations and get too comfortable in that role. For example, they start broadcasting information from a client's organization, and someone in the organization finds out about it. Then there's trouble. It's wise to always consider yourself an outsider, no matter how friendly relations are.

WHAT DOES IT ALL MEAN?

Information usually comes from the grapevine in a pretty raw state. Let's go back to that grapevine message, "Kramer canned." No one has bothered interpreting in detail what Kramer's firing could mean to you. No one may have thought through how Kramer's firing will affect your department or the organization in general. To dig down to what it all means, you may have to consult what I like to call the "Greek Chorus." All types of people belong to the Greek Chorus of a company. What all these people have in common is enough time at the company to have a unique perspective, wisdom about organization machinations, no ax to grind, and discretion. Just as in the Greek dramas of old, the organization's Greek Chorus will usually articulate the truth of the situation. The Chorus may interpret "Kramer canned" in any number of ways:

- A precedent has been set, since no one has been fired at General Manufacturing since 1975
- Management is attempting to get a message out: *No one is indispensable*
- The door is now open to younger people breaking into senior management—if they want to go after Kramer's job

• Headquarters is now all-powerful, and the authority of the subsidiaries has been greatly weakened

If you want the reality behind the headlines, make friends with at least one member of the Greek Chorus. You will know who they are. Everyone respects them and their judgment. One way to make friends of these people is to bring them information they may not have access to. Approach the giving of information casually: "Oh, by the way, did you hear . . ."

GETTING ZAPPED

Believe me, it's happened to all of us. You said you were sorry that Kramer got fired, but it's traveling the grapevine that you're *not* sorry Kramer got fired—and people want to know what you have against Kramer. Or you only told one person you were job hunting—and you're *sure* it's not that person who's the leak—but this morning your boss asked you why you're looking for another job.

Why do these things happen, and what can you do about it? You can get zapped for a number of reasons, all of them curable.

Perhaps you trusted too quickly. Remember, *everyone* has an agenda. And someone's agenda may involve squashing you, or getting dirt from your department and passing it on. That's why you need to be cautious with what you say—and especially with e-mail. Once you hit "send," you lose all control over its ultimate destination; anyone can forward your message to anyone else. Always remember that e-mail is a form of public communication.

Or maybe you shared your feelings too freely. Work isn't your Wednesday-night support group. You can't expect everyone at the office to be on the lookout for your interests. There are times when your coworkers not only couldn't care less, they might actually use the material against you.

There are creatures in any organization who excel in the art of pumping others for information and passing it on. They include:

The Good Mothers. These poisonous entities prey on people who are either new to an organization or in a crisis. On the surface, they are warm and caring. They use a concerned tone when they speak with you. They seem sympathetic as they probe for information, making comments such as, "It must be difficult to work for a controller like Maxine," or, "You must be getting pretty burned out by all that overtime." Be friendly with these people, but say nothing you wouldn't announce over the loudspeaker.

Moles. Find out who the moles are. These insecure creeps believe the only way they can survive in an organization is to bring dirt back to the boss. They will take you to lunch and quiz you about every aspect of your job. It's politically astute to go to lunch with them if they ask you to, but focus only on positive aspects of your job. If you don't reveal something negative, they'll get frustrated. Eventually they'll stop pumping you.

The Embittered. They have an ax to grind. Maybe they were passed over for a promotion because they didn't have an MBA. Maybe the person who brought them into the organization was fired. Maybe they perceive that others are getting more travel opportunities than they are. So they try to create havoc at work. They do this by plugging misleading information into the grapevine. If they find a reason to dislike you or resent you, you could be a victim. The good news is that it's easy to spot these troublemakers: They're the ones with the visible chips on their shoulders. The bad news is that you might have to do some damage control if they make you a target.

DAMAGE CONTROL

There's a misleading rumor on the grapevine, and this time it's about you. What do you do? Well, the worst thing to do is nothing. Your silence reinforces the credibility of the rumor.

The best approach is to involve intermediaries. Get other people to do your dirty work. The simple fact that they're standing up for you will look good. Also, they can help replace the rumor with the truth. Often these intermediaries will be your friends at work. Other times mere acquaintances will be willing to go to bat for you. Maybe they dislike your enemy. Maybe this happened to them before. Maybe they think you got a raw deal. Whatever their reasons, if they help you, thank them. You owe them big-time.

You can also fight back on your own. Go to the biggest talkers in the organization and tell them that you heard a rumor about you, and, since it contained wrong information, you'd like to clear up the misunderstanding. Then tell your version of the story. Be calm; the calmer you are, the more credible you'll seem. Simply explain the facts. Try not to place blame; blaming others might get you involved in a battle, when all you want to do is get the facts straight.

GETTING BACK ON YOUR FEET

In this erratic new world of professional life, people are getting tangled up in the grapevine more and more often. Maybe they didn't make their quota this quarter. Maybe the whole department is in trouble for going over budget. Maybe they were passed over for a promotion. They're embarrassed, and they figure everyone is talking about them. And maybe everyone is.

If this happens to you, what should you do? Well, as Woody Allen famously said, 80 percent of success is just showing up. And it's especially true when you've suffered a reversal. In western Pennsylvania, a state senator's administrative assistant ran for local office and lost the election. She didn't come in to work the next day. The grapevine had a field day talking about her lack of courage. And she never recovered. So, first of all, show up.

Second, if you were wrong, or if you're responsible for what went wrong, admit it publicly. There's no need to overdo this and confess your every minor sin to the world. Just admit what happened. For example, a writer was abrupt with a secretary. The secretary told everyone in the office about this rudeness. The writer told the biggest talkers in the organization that she had been abrupt with the secretary and regretted it. She also apologized to the secretary. She didn't, however, go into an explanation of her tendency to be impatient. Say enough but not too much.

Third, insert your upcoming plans into the grapevine. Mention your plan, to cite one possible example, to make or surpass your quota over the next quarter. That will encourage the organization to look at your future rather than your past.

YOUR CHAMPIONS

If you get lucky, someone—or perhaps several people—in the organization may become your champion on the grapevine. This happened at an auto company to a young woman who had just moved to the Midwest from New York. A director was attracted to her brashness and intelligence. He praised her to a few colleagues. Although she was new, her reputation for being an outstanding strategic thinker spread quickly.

To attract champions, try to be where the executives are. Volunteer for task forces, even if they're for corny things like the fiftieth anniversary of the company. Or try to "adopt" a champion. If you speak well of Bert, he'll speak well of you. This arrangement is most effective if you're not known to be friends already.

YOUR VALUES

The grapevine isn't amoral. Keith Davis tells a story about some executives who weren't invited to a company social function. Most of them never heard about the party, either before or after the event. That is, people who participate in the grapevine often have scruples and hesitate to reveal information that might hurt someone.

But that isn't to say the grapevine can't get nasty. At the organization formerly called International Harvester, bonus time came for the executives right in the middle of a strike. Chief executive officer Archie McCardell was advised not to take a large bonus, at least not while the strikers were suffering. McCardell ignored the advice. To many people, he came to represent the bad guy. Eventually he lost his job. He became a casualty of his own greed—and of the grapevine.

If you want to feel good about yourself during the day and be able to sleep at night, you will need to develop a set of values for dealing with the grapevine. You have to establish the rules for yourself. When I was in my first job, I knew that I had to write down the grapevine rules I would follow. I follow these same rules today. They are:

- If anyone begins a negative discussion about a friend of mine, I promptly make it clear that the person is a friend and I'm not comfortable discussing this. Sometimes I add positive information about my friend.
- If negative information comes my way about someone— even an enemy—and I know it's not true, I set the record straight. And I hope that someone will do the same for me.
- If I hear that there's erroneous information floating around about me, I try to track down the source. If I can't find the source, I still fight back, using both intermediaries and my own direct input.
- I always help people new to the organization adjust to the grapevine.

You can create rules for yourself. The list needn't be long. You can control your relationship with the grapevine.

Things to Remember

- The grapevine is a "must" in professional life
- Anyone can learn to work the grapevine
- Don't trust too easily
- If attacked, fight back
- Create your own code of conduct for dealing with the grapevine

6

NETWORKING

This chapter is must reading IF:

- You want a better job
- You need more information about what's going on in your organization and field of expertise
- You want to get support from others
- You feel all alone

Over and over again, networking has proved to be a dynamite tool for finding jobs, lobbying for a promotion, lining up new business, finding out what's going on in your organization, getting competitive intelligence about your industry, brainstorming solutions for problems, creating a support group, and being of service to other people.

You can network on the Internet, on the phone, on the 6:02 AM commuter train, in the cafeteria at work, in associations, in clubs, at church, in your condo's laundromat, in the supermarket, at trade shows, on elevators, in restrooms, on the line to see a movie, at your daughter's dance recital, and just about anywhere people congregate. In essence, all networking is, is reaching out to another person.

MASTER NETWORKERS

One master networker and multitalented man is John Kao, who has an MBA from Harvard and an MD in psychiatry from Yale. A strategic advisor to individuals, cities, and nations, he taught at Harvard for fourteen years, is chairman of the Institute for Large Scale Innovation, authored *Innovation Nation,* was executive producer of the movie *Sex, Lies, and Videotape,* and more. He knows thousands of people, but it's the quality and diversity of those contacts that counts, not the quantity. As *The Economist* notes, Kao's networking genius is that he can bring different worlds together. That's what networking does: It enables you to connect not only with people in your field but also with those far beyond its confines. By networking effectively, you can expand your perspective in a way that would otherwise be nearly impossible.

Another master networker is President Bill Clinton, who has been called the "networking president." Even at Oxford, where he was a Rhodes scholar, he was networking. When he met people, he would enter their names in a little black address book along with a few relevant details about them. He wanted to make sure he wouldn't forget them. That's a quality he shares with George W. Bush. At Yale, Bush was an indifferent student, but his ability to remember names and faces was unsurpassed.

Orlando Camargo is another networking pro. He was about to go to graduate school when he heard about an opportunity to teach English for a year in Japan and jumped at it. "That turned into twenty-seven years," he told me. In Japan, he became vice president and director of corporate communications for Goldman Sachs and, later, president of Ogilvy PR Worldwide Japan. Now working with the Dilenschneider Group, he is fluent in Japanese, Spanish, English, and American Sign Language and is a skilled networker with a special expertise in social media strategies.

Here's what he had to say when I interviewed him:

INTERVIEW: ORLANDO CAMARGO

RLD: What is networking, and has it changed due to social media?

OC: At the core, it has never changed. It's always, at its base, a meeting with another human being to share something and hopefully to have them appreciate you a little bit more. It's about establishing your worth and your credibility and exchanging information and letting the process take it from there. To network effectively, you have to sell yourself in a way that doesn't seem like you're selling yourself. For young people now, the hope is that they don't rely only on social media but that they supplement it with person-to-person contact.

RLD: How can you sell yourself and not look as if that's what you're doing?

OC: It all comes down to what your grandmother told you: Just be yourself. Be natural. You can express ambition, but show who you are without pretension.

RLD: Can you do that through the social media?

OC: Yes. In the new social media environment, it's important to brand yourself in a public way in order to be recognized, and you have to take charge of your brand. Begin with something neutral, which means, as we used to say in PR, nothing that you would not want on the front page of the *New York Times*. Start with your interests and whatever it is that you do professionally. It could be as simple as a Facebook entry and a LinkedIn page that describes you and your background in a way that cannot be misconstrued. Another strategy is to have a blog that expresses your skill sets, hobbies, or ambitions and gives a view of your life and how you see it.

RLD: What about Twitter?

OC: It's not for everybody. If you're going to talk about what you had for breakfast, that's not the best use of your time. But if it is coordinated with thoughtful blog entries and a purposeful LinkedIn profile, by all means use Twitter. Do it in a way that represents you honestly and transparently without overdoing it and without going too much into your private life.

RLD: Does old-fashioned networking still have a role?

OC: Absolutely. All the social media activity makes face-to-face contact more relevant and more humanizing. Because of the social media, some people are forgetting basic social skills. You can never forget those social skills, because it's all about communicating and connecting.

RLD: What is the worst mistake that young people make in networking?

OC: It's misrepresenting yourself by getting ahead of who you really are and trying to project something that is not there yet, which is very different from expressing an ambition or an aspiration. The basics don't change: Be yourself. Keep up with people. Interact with them. Don't forget to call back. And send a thank-you note when someone has helped you; people will remember you for that. Some people think it's enough to say thanks with an e-mail or a tweet without doing anything in addition. That's not the case.

RLD: What should they do then, besides sending a note?

OC: They can do many simple things. For example, they should read and comment on the other person's blog and become involved with that person's brand or activities, as you would with any individual you're interested in. That's what networking is—an exchange of views and ideas. It's all about engagement. It's not just about making the contact. It's what you do after the initial meeting. It's the effort to get to know that person genuinely. Most people will naturally reciprocate.

RLD: If you were to give three networking tips, what would they be?

OC: Number one: Be in charge of your brand. If you Google yourself, make sure the results include content you created. Number two: Engage and follow up; don't just connect. And number three: Move away from your screen. Pick up the phone or speak with the person face-to-face. Human contact creates amazing networking opportunities and results.

RLD: I agree. Nothing beats personal contact.

THE RIGHT ATTITUDE

Networking is more than a technique to get ahead. Networking springs from an attitude that says: *I want to be of help to someone who needs it.* That explains why too many people get nothing substantial from networking. They have an attitude, but the wrong one. They take little interest in the needs of others. They're in it solely for themselves.

Ted H. was one of those. He was on the phone every evening talking to me and my colleagues about how we could help him get a job. We helped him with his résumé and cover letter. We coached him in how to present himself in interviews. After each interview, we led him through the postmortem on how it went. Well, Ted H. did get a job. And we never heard from him until he was out of work again. We wrote him off as a bad debt.

When you reach out, you have to be prepared both to receive and to give. Networking is one of mankind's oldest bartering systems. If I help you get a job, you might help me get my mother into a nursing home. If you coach me on how to ask for a raise, I'll share my fishing secrets with you. If you listen to me whine about my boss, I'll listen to you whine about your boss. The core of networking is give-and-take.

In a year, some of us build up a large debt on the network. Sometimes we have to be creative in how to repay that debt. One man gives lavish parties. One woman gives expensive gifts at holiday time. I usually like to pay off my debt by doing a favor for someone.

HOW NETWORKING OPERATES

Networking has its own rules. You have to know them. Here's how you should operate.

Create headlines. Just as it does on the grapevine, information travels networks in the form of headlines. "Joe out of work—again." "Marcia retooling herself." "Jan in carpet-cleaning business." "Paul offering new investment vehicles." "Frank has new job." These little nuggets of information travel quickly, which is why it's smart to be proactive by deciding on the message you want to convey and preparing your own headline. Don't leave it to the group to create a headline for you.

Before you go someplace to network, figure out what a useful headline would be for you. If you're changing careers from teaching to sales, your headline shouldn't be "Caroline awarding-winning teacher." That locks you into the past. An appropriate headline would be "Caroline interested in sales." If your situation changes—say, you switch from looking for a job to opening your own business—you would also change your headline. Practice saying your headline before you actually network. Your presentation should be short—twenty seconds maximum.

Look at the long term. The worst way to start networking is this: You find yourself out of a job, you go to your Facebook page for the first time in months, you decide to post your résumé on LinkedIn, and you commit to joining a professional group for a month. Sorry. That simply won't work. The best time to join a network is when things are going great.

Like investing in the stock market, networking is a long-term activity. You can't just parachute in and expect results from people who don't really know you. If you haven't helped anyone, if you haven't performed service on behalf of a group, you're out there on your own. Networking is about giving as well as receiving.

Network online. Join LinkedIn, Facebook, Twitter, as well as networks geared to your field—and participate actively. But don't allow yourself to remain glued to an electronic screen every moment of the day. The most powerful form of networking occurs face-to-face.

Join groups. Not virtual groups—actual groups that meet in real rooms. And remember that there are rarely quick hits in networking. Ellen Volpe, president of American Business Associates of Long Island, observes that "networking is not selling." You're not looking for an order but, rather, for a relationship.

That's why it's off-putting to have a new group member methodically survey the room and target the people who are "must-talks." Again, networking is not sales. You're not there to get an order. You're there to develop relationships over time. These relationships will lead you to other people you ought to know. It may take a while. When you join that organization and network, don't expect great results right away.

Keep work networks separate from outside networks. One offers depth; the other provides perspective. You need both—the kind you find in the office and the kind you find in the community. In an outside network you're bound to get more emotional support. You can't expect that inside your organization. Even though there's a lot of rhetoric about teamwork, when a promotion comes up, only one person gets it.

Do your homework before you go to the group. If I'm going to a general gathering, I make sure that I listen to a news program beforehand. The national and local news is something I should know, anyway, and it's often a good icebreaker. If I'm having lunch with a judge, I first do a literature search about current judicial matters. This enables me to ask intelligent questions.

Management consultant Mickey Veich points out that networking is more than looking good and passing out business cards. "Asking questions is very important, especially the right ones," says Veich. He adds that doing your homework, so that you can ask the right questions, can make or break your networking efforts.

Volunteer. There are two types of service. One type is helping out individuals. The other type is helping out the organization. Both will enhance your reputation. Also, by working with other group members, you greatly expand your network. That's because those members may introduce you to people in *their* networks. In addition, by volunteering, you may have the opportunity to get to know people you might not normally meet, including members of the group's inner circle. They could have powerful contacts.

Be a reliable source of information. Before you tell the unemployed writer in the group that General Widget is hiring two writers, recheck that this is true. If you're not sure your source is reliable, then admit that. Inaccurate information builds false hopes and damages your own credibility.

Learn to work grapevines. Every group has a grapevine. You want to get plugged into it. The best way to do that is to be visible in the group. Once they see that you truly are part of the group, they will begin to share information with you. Be cool while you're waiting to be accepted. Don't ask too many pointed questions, and do share the information you do have.

Be aware of your image. In networking, says Lillian Bjorseth, a networking consultant in Chicago, people make up their minds about you in ten seconds. In those ten seconds they've made many decisions about your character, success, heritage, economic level, education, sophistication, and trustworthiness.

In short, in ten seconds people respond to your image. You want that image to highlight your strengths and mask your weaknesses. Use your ten seconds well.

Show grace under pressure. Great leaders and great people are known for their grace under pressure. No matter which crisis they have at the office or at home, they don't conduct themselves in ways that will upset or annoy others. That's the way you want to be, even if the boss is berating you or you just lost your job. Loss of control and desperation are unwelcome in any network. And you will be perceived as desperate if you frantically go around the room and introduce yourself to massive numbers of people.

Things to Remember

- Networking is a multipurpose tool
- Networking is about helping others, not only yourself
- Networking is about relationships
- Networking is a long-term activity
- Showing grace under pressure is always a plus

7

MAKING ALLIES
OF YOUR ELDERS

This chapter is must reading IF:

- You hate or fear the older generation
- Members of the older generation are uncomfortable with you
- The older generation has the power in your office
- It seems you have nothing in common with your elders

The "Generation Gap" became famous in the 1960s when "Don't trust anyone over thirty" was the mantra of the young, and the divide between generations seemed to be a chasm. In fact, conflict between generations is nothing new. It is as old as the mother-in-law and daughter-in-law who can't get along. And did any of us, after the age of about fourteen, ever really get along with our parents?

FOUR GENERATIONS

Right now in the United States, there are up to four generations in the workplace, each with its own experiences, values, and styles. There are Traditionalists, sometimes called the Silent Generation or the Greatest Generation, born between 1900 and 1945; Baby Boomers, born between 1946 and 1964; members of Generation X, born between 1965 and 1980; and members of Generation Y, also known as Millennials, who were born between 1981 and 2000. Depending on who's doing the counting, you can add or subtract a few years in most of these categories.

In subtle ways, or in blatantly obvious ways, each generation usually disparages the generations that have come before or after. It reminds me of the old song in which parents wonder why kids can't be like they were—perfect in every way. But it is possible not only to get along but to be allies with members of another generation. In this chapter, I'll explain how you can make allies of your elders.

MY RUN-INS

At work in the 1960s, I had my own private hell with the older generation. I stood out because I was an eager beaver. That made me a target for the elders to vent their spleen upon. I had to learn quickly how to handle it.

For example, there was a Pulitzer Prize–winning journalist associated with our public relations office. His day job was working on an East Coast newspaper. Seemingly out of nowhere, this award-winning writer came up to me one day and said, "You want to get ahead. Well, it won't be on my back." I was stunned, but I didn't scurry back to my desk and hide underneath it. If I had let him see my fear, this man would have tormented me forever. I told him I thought it was possible for us to have a good working relationship. I held out an olive branch that could help him save face. He went for it, and we worked together very well. Lessons learned: *Don't let them know you're scared. And don't give up on the possibility of a friendship with another generation.*

There was another incident when I was working on the Columbia University public relations account during the student riots in 1968. At the end of the riots, Grayson Kirk, Columbia's president, and David Truman, the chair of the trustees, came to me and thanked me for what I had done for the university. I was only twentysomething, and this was a big deal to me. What came next was an even bigger deal. They asked if they could have my telephone number in case they needed to reach me over the weekend. No one knew whether the riots would break out again.

The following Monday I was called in by my supervisor, Bob C. He was much older than I, the same type you may be dealing with now. Bob C. cursed at me. He got all red in the face. He wagged his finger. He told me that I was trying to steal his day in the sun. As his rage ran its course, I realized two things. One, when I was asked for my telephone number, I should also have offered Bob's telephone number. Two, I didn't have to take this abuse from him. I thought about that and went up a level to see Bob C.'s boss. It worked. Bob C.'s boss spoke to Bob, and never again did he wag his finger at me. Lessons learned: *First of all, no matter how cautious you are, you're going to make mistakes dealing with another generation. Second, you don't have to put up with bad behavior. Third, find an effective way to try to stop the abuse.*

TALKIN' 'BOUT MY GENERATION

"Crabbed age and youth cannot live together," wrote William Shakespeare. The question is, can they work together? Because it is a rare organization that does not include members of several generations.

TRADITIONALISTS

Given their age, you might think that Traditionalists would be an endangered species in the workplace. But that's not the case. When the economy is bad, even the elderly can't afford to retire—and some who can clearly prefer not to. (Think of Warren Buffett or Clint Eastwood.) In 2012, according to Labor Department statistics, more than 10 percent of men and about

5 percent of women over seventy-five were still working. One of them could easily be your boss—and that wouldn't be the worst thing in the world. This generation is known for stability, loyalty, and dedication: the old-fashioned values. They obey the rules and expect you to do the same. But they're often allergic to risk, uncomfortable with change, and—as you probably know—inept with technology.

BABY BOOMERS

I'm a member of the Silent Generation, that subset of the Traditionalist generation that came of age in the conformist 1950s. But emotionally and in terms of my worldview, I feel like a Baby Boomer. If you understand Baby Boomers, I think you'll find it easier to put up with them—and even enjoy them.

Whereas Traditionalists were born during an era of crisis, the first Baby Boomers were born during the euphoria that followed World War II. In many ways, Boomers might be considered the luckiest generation, for they grew up in a time of great prosperity and high expectations. After World War II, when much of the world was in shambles, the United States was experiencing record economic growth. Per capita income in the 1950s grew by 48 percent, and 60 percent of the population fit into the category called "middle class."

If you were a young person in the 1950s, the United States was close to utopia. The family unit was still intact, and families were so child-centered they even took their vacations where the little ones could enjoy themselves. TV was new, and it had special programming for children, such as the *Howdy Doody* show. Because of Boomers' sheer numbers—79.4 million of them—the world had to accommodate them. There were new playgrounds, new schools, new hospitals, all built just for them—and they knew it. The media made them celebrities. Whatever fad they were into made the cover of *Time*. In response to all this attention, Boomers began to assume they were special.

For Baby Boomers, education was widely available, of excellent quality, and affordable. Baby Boomers thought nothing of going to graduate school after four years of college. They are probably the most highly educated generation in American history.

In addition, many of them were students during an extremely contentious period—the cultural upheavals of the 1960s. Some Boomers embraced those movements with gusto. They campaigned for civil rights and against the Vietnam War, rigid sexual mores, and the values that their parents brought with them from the Great Depression. They got to feel very righteous about their own point of view. Plus, while they were trying to change the world, they had a ball experimenting with different lifestyles and listening to a lot of exciting music.

When it came time for them to finally enter the workforce, they once again wanted it all. And they were sure they were going to get it all: easily available work that was also interesting; promotions; a loving, supportive family who didn't interfere with the job; the ability to grow on the job; and money—a lot of it. The "Great American Job Machine" was cranking out plenty of new positions; there were more than enough jobs to go around, even for the many young women who entered the workforce on a large scale for the first time. Both men and women went to organizations like GM or GE and planned their strategies for climbing the corporate ladder. Many of them made it to middle management. Some of them made it to the top.

Along the way, there were recessions, notably in 1974–75 and 1981–82. Some Boomers lost jobs. But they were able to get new ones, and often better ones, before too long. Their generation still had its magic—until downsizing came along in the late 1980s. That changed everything. Overnight the Boomers went from smug, well-paid executives to vulnerable working stiffs who could be out of a job at any time. For the first time in their lives, they were vulnerable to layoffs. For the first time, they felt fear.

And it wasn't that easy anymore to get another job. There was simply less opportunity out there than there had been when they were young. Harvard Business School professor Rosabeth Moss Kanter cites a Fortune Magazine study of managers who lost their jobs in 1986. For about 75 percent of them, there was economic hardship. Some laid-off Baby Boomers found they couldn't get another comparable job. Others found it took them a long time to find another job—or, at the new job, they had to take a pay cut. In addition, downsizing brought about a flatter corporate organization and less upward mobility. Many Boomers had to face the fact that where they were was the best they'd ever do. And those lucky enough to still have jobs kept looking over their shoulders for the ax. It was heartbreaking to see their grandiose expectations crumble.

As a group, women of the Baby Boom generation suffered an additional crisis. They were finding how difficult it was to have it all. And despite their talent, drive, and sacrifices, they were bumping up against the glass ceiling.

The 1990s, presided over by über-Boomer Bill Clinton, saw some economic improvement and were a better time for the Boomers. The twenty-first century has been less kind. In 2007, just as the oldest among them were looking forward to retirement, the economy took a sharp turn downward—and the recovery proved distressingly slow. The Great Recession was hard on everyone. But for Boomers, once the golden generation, it was more than a financial disaster. For them, it felt like a betrayal. Life wasn't supposed to be this way.

GENERATION X

The Baby Boomers grew up in a secure, Ozzie-and-Harriet world. Their children, the members of Generation X, had a different experience. They were born into a world of diminished expectations, of layoffs and downsizing, and their lives have been anything but golden. Most GenXers never knew the Great American Jobs Machine that had sustained the Boomers.

Many suffered through their parents' divorces. Many of them lived with a single mother struggling with poverty. Many of them were latchkey kids. Many had to take on part-time jobs at a young age. By the time they were ready for college, inflation had turned a four-year education into a six-figure investment. Some of them are still paying off their student loans.

Not surprisingly, their attitude is often cynical, their style sometimes ironic. They roll their eyes at the Boomers' desire to change the world. It doesn't strike them as idealistic; it strikes them as naïve. Nor do they admire the workaholic tendencies of so many Boomers. They reject that obsession (and are therefore sometimes described as Slackers). Actually, it's not that they aren't willing to work. I employ many of them, and I can tell you, their work ethic is equal to anyone's. It's just that they value their personal lives—and their friends—as much as their careers. They are also the first generation to feel truly comfortable with diversity. They seem at home in the big world, not just their little slice of it. That's something I admire about them.

GENERATION Y

As I write, many members of Generation Y are still too young to drive, to vote, to join the military, to enter the labor market. But those who are in their twenties and early thirties have already made an impact in the workplace.

That's because they have certain qualities that almost guarantee success. Confidence is one. Sociability is another. Diversity is second nature to them. They are the most global generation we've ever seen. They are innovative, optimistic, and entrepreneurial. And they're all digital natives. It's no accident that some of the most notable businesses in recent years are those with young people at the helm. Facebook's Mark Zuckerberg is far from the only one. I expect these kids to change the world.

MAKING FRIENDS AND ALLIES

Each generation has its own style, its own positive qualities, and its own set of foibles. The most successful people know how to bypass those idiosyncrasies and connect with members of every generation. How can you do that? Begin by having a little compassion. Take the Traditionalists, for example. They may have lived through the Great Depression, stormed the beach at Normandy, or presided over the most successful economy this world has ever seen. But that was then. This is now. Despite their vast experience, they're at the end of their careers, and they know it. So what can you do to get along with them? Offer technological help. And ask their advice. They may know less than nothing about Tumblr or online dating, but they know their field. They know what has worked historically and what has not, and you may be surprised at how willing they are to share their insights. If you approach them in a friendly way, they will go out of their way to help you. You might even consider asking a Traditionalist to mentor you.

The same is true for Baby Boomers, only more so. After all, Traditionalists always knew that life could be tough. They were born to be grown-ups. Not so the Boomers. They thought life would be an adventure, filled with rewards. The hard-driving Type As who went into business expected to conquer every obstacle they encountered. Others planned on a safari of self-discovery, at the end of which they would reach enlightenment. Neither group succeeded. Now, they've lost their belief that the world can be made perfect, and many are in financial trouble. What's more, they're shocked by the aging process and afraid of being out of touch. What can you do? Treat them as friends; Boomers really care about the nature of a relationship. Be willing to listen to their opinions. And if you feel for them, steer them to what's new and interesting. Discuss an article you read; send them the link. Take them to your favorite lunch spot. Offer technical expertise. Introduce them to Pandora or Spotify or other apps you think they'd like. They will be delighted. And keep in mind: they're still in power. The youngest Baby Boomers won't turn sixty-five until 2029. You need them— and vice versa.

GenXers in many ways fashioned themselves in opposition to the Boomers. They were determined not to make the same mistakes, so they maintained a skeptical distance and a certain level of distrust. Which means that, if you want to connect with them, you'd better not be seen as a taker or as someone determined to climb the corporate ladder at any cost. That will not impress them. They value good times and time off, and they expect you to have a life outside the office. You can help them by being a team player, being fun to be around, and offering creative suggestions. Keep your plans to conquer the world to yourself. Raw ambition will not endear you to them.

If someone from Generation Y figures heavily in your professional life, you're in luck, especially if you're also a member of Generation Y. They have the same optimism that the Baby Boomers once had, and they expect to accomplish a lot. Your ambition will not disturb them in the least (unless it's directed at them in a competitive way). They will respect you for being goal-oriented, and they won't care how numerous your goals may be. They love variety, and they're multitaskers. But remember, they're impatient and easily bored. Act accordingly. And always be positive in their presence. Don't tell them what *won't* work. They want to know what *will*.

Having friends and allies in every age group will expand your options enormously. It will give you insights you'd never get from hanging around only with your cohorts. And it will feel good.

Things to Remember

- Generational strife has always existed
- If you understand who people are, you can learn to like them

- Everyone wants to connect with other people
- Be compassionate toward other generations; don't disparage their experiences
- Helping others is the best way to make allies

8

IMAGE

This chapter is must reading IF:

- You are in a crisis
- Somebody has damaged your image
- You feel you need an image fix
- You don't know what your image is

Whether you like it or not, agree with it or not, think it's unfair or not, people judge you by your image.

At one time Lance Armstrong, a cancer survivor who won the Tour de France bicycle race seven times, was an inspiration to many people. Then he was accused of taking performance-enhancing drugs and banned from the sport for life. His reputation plummeted.

Democrat John Edwards used to be a rising star. In 2004 he was nominated for vice president, and everyone thought he might run for president in the next election. Then the *National Enquirer* published an article alleging that he was having an extramarital affair under especially ugly circumstances. The scandal spiraled out of control. His political career was over, his image ruined.

Every young person starting out in a job has an image. If

you're not satisfied with that image, or you've outgrown it, you can change it.

There is no such thing as not having an image. If you think you don't have an image, then what people are probably saying about you is this: You're neither here nor there, you're wishy-washy, and you are indifferent to the world around you. I knew a man who had a PhD in philosophy. He was a near genius. But he didn't take pains with his image. Around the office his nickname was "The Unmade Bed." For all his intelligence and drive, he didn't get anywhere. In fact, he was let go in the first wave of layoffs.

If you don't consciously create your image, that image will be formed primarily by the impressions of people who work with you. That's giving a lot of power to people who might not have your best interests uppermost in their minds. Not cultivating an image puts you on the defensive, instead of where you should be—on the offensive. The Republican Party has an image. The Democratic Party has an image. Chris Christie has an image. Barack Obama has an image. The mail boy has an image. And if those people haven't given a lot of thought to that image, they're not very savvy.

Image starts early. A speech I delivered in 1972 is now on the Internet. My image was starting to develop way back then—I just didn't realize it.

WHAT IS IMAGE?

Your image is the bundle of signals you give off. Your image includes just about everything: your clothes, your manners and your mannerisms, the music you listen to, the cell phone you use, the movies you see, the language you use, the suggestions you make at meetings.

Your image works effectively only if it's integrated. For example, suppose you wear conservative suits and are meticulous in your work but overly gregarious and sloppy in your personal manner. That discontinuity would confuse people. In managing your image, you don't want your appearance to say one thing and your behavior to say another.

Also, there shouldn't be major incongruities between what your image is inside the office and what your image is in the community. That will also confuse people. They may even think that you are unstable.

You might say that your image is a shorthand way of telling the world what you're about. Conan O'Brien's image says: "I'm a nice guy—and also pretty funny."

Bill Clinton's image says: "Like me." Actress Lindsay Lohan's image says: "I've been through the wringer."

What is your image saying? Maybe you should ask a friend about this.

And, as Roger Ailes, President of Fox News and media adviser to US presidents and to corporate CEOs, always stresses: folks make up their mind about your image almost instantly.

I can't tell you the number of times I've gone into CEOs' offices knowing I have a very brief time to make my pitch—and my impression. Those CEOs don't see "Bob Dilenschneider, good citizen and entrepreneur." As I'm sitting there making my pitch, they see "a management consultant who can or cannot help me." If the CEOs decide that I can't help them, they make that decision fast—and have been known to bid me "good day" and walk out of the room! Somehow, my image didn't communicate "can be of use to you," and there's nothing I can do to change that impression or pry loose that piece of business. It's primarily my image that gets, or doesn't get, me new business. Fortunately, most times my image communicates to clients: "Yes, I'm the one to help you."

IT'S A BIG WORLD OUT THERE

Image can differ around the world. In the northeastern United States, people tend to be aggressive but formal. In the Pacific Northwest, people tend to be laid-back and casual. And you need to know such things before you go there and present yourself. Years ago in California there was tremendous criticism about the "pushy" New Yorkers who had moved there. By now native-born Californians have adjusted to the New York style. But I still have to tone down my drive and slow down my pace when I go to Los Angeles or San Francisco.

One hard-charging woman went to a utility company in L.A. for a job interview. Nothing in her résumé indicated she was born and raised in Brooklyn, but the interviewer, who hates New Yorkers, cut the interview short and didn't even have her meet his boss. She never had a chance.

Overseas, the challenge can be the same. If you're going to do business in China, you have to project a different image than you would in Japan. Moreover, the image that you would ideally want to project in Beijing will not be the same as the one that would succeed in Shanghai. In Italy, I'm relaxed. In France, I'm more formal. The world may be a global village, but regional differences persist.

IMAGES IN PROFESSIONS

In law school or medical school, you not only learn a profession, you become socialized in how to act appropriately in those fields. In your first few months at GE or McKinsey Consulting, you will also be socialized to conform to those organizations' images. In the seminary, a young man training to be a Roman Catholic priest learns how to comport himself in a priestly manner.

If you enter a profession and don't bother to adapt to the overall image in the field, or you resist adapting to it, you're going to be in trouble. Some mavericks, such as Sir Richard Branson of the Virgin Group, manage to get away with it, but they're usually outstanding at what they do.

As a public relations strategist, I am expected to be gregarious and sure of myself. If I were introverted and insecure, people would be puzzled at first, then angry that I had violated their expectations. Wouldn't you be annoyed if your doctor relentlessly goofed around instead of acting like a medical professional?

Professional image brings with it a set of expectations. You have to be willing—and able—to conform to those expectations.

CHANGING TIMES

Your image will probably change with the times. It might also change if you switch jobs or if your organization adopts a new type of corporate culture. In a small trade association you might get away with looking like an absentminded professor. In a traditional consumer products company you would need to appear professional and serious. But if a new CEO came in as a change agent, you might want to appear more energetic and put in more "face time" with clients. Part of Madonna's marketing genius is that she can sense when it's time to change her image.

When I first started out in business, the prevailing image for an ambitious man was an energetic persona. You had to be careful not to become too energetic, though, because that could lead people to think you were not entirely focused or in control. For a woman, once she was married, the prevailing image was that of partner and helpmeet to her husband. She could have other interests, such as art or charity work or even a job, but her "core competency" was helping Mr. Man.

How all that has changed! Being energetic is no longer enough. In addition to earning a living, ambitious men are now expected to be sensitive, intuitive, concerned about the world, and helpful to others. And although some men may still see women primarily in terms of their personal relationships, more is expected of them too. In the workplace women are expected to be as ambitious, driven, and self-sufficient as their male colleagues.

As in the world at large, gender issues in the workplace are far from being resolved, for men or for women. How sensitive ought I, a man, be? If my client loses a job, should we both sit down and shed a few tears? Must a woman, to be perceived as "feminine," still bring in home-baked cookies? Or would doing so undercut her professional image? My best take on all this is that both sexes should avoid playing into stereotypes. On Monday I shouldn't spend the day saying how I can't wait until *Monday Night Football,* and women shouldn't feel that they *must* talk about their children. Neither should show favoritism based on gender. What counts is performance. I've rarely seen a manager fail who has consistently rewarded performance.

OUT IN THE OPEN

At one time in society, we didn't talk openly about image; that seemed too manipulative. You were expected to pick up the right way to present yourself from the way your parents conducted themselves. That's primarily why people from professional families were so successful back then: They knew the rules. They knew how to present themselves. They knew enough not to discuss business at the office Christmas party.

Back then, if your bosses were doing your annual review and noticed something they didn't like in your image, they might recommend that you be more "businesslike." You had to figure out what they meant.

Again, things have changed since then. Today, everyone talks about image. The conversation may begin with "dressing for success," but it seldom ends there. Clothing and grooming matter, of course: Optics count. But today's image consultants and coaches can also help you fine-tune your body language; speak more effectively; master proper business behavior, including the appropriate etiquette for all things digital; make an entrance; shake hands correctly; project confidence; and develop your own professional brand.

BENEFITS OF A GOOD IMAGE

With image, the stakes are high. That's because image is the foundation of success—both for big companies like Colgate-Palmolive and for individuals like you. I work with many organizations that want "just the right image." When they get it, it directly affects their bottom line. In *Reputation: Realizing Value from the Corporate Image,* Charles Fombrun points out that a good image allows organizations to:

- Charge premium prices for their products
- Achieve stability in revenues
- Pay lower prices for purchases
- Attract top people to work at the organization
- Obtain greater loyalty from employees and customers
- Receive greater latitude to act by constituents
- Encounter fewer crises

For you, as an individual, the benefits of a good image can also be profound. I've seen young people with good images enjoy:

- **The halo effect.** Everything you do is viewed with an expectation that it will be excellent.
- **Increased latitude to act.** The powers-that-be don't keep you on a short leash.
- **More money.** For example, Susan Bixler in *The Professional Image* cites a study by Judith Walters of Fairleigh Dickinson University. The study focused on professional appearance. "Before" (that is, not highly professional-looking) and "after" (that is, highly professional-looking) photos with identical résumés were sent to more than one thousand companies. The recipients were asked to determine a starting salary for the person in the photo. The "after" pictures were assigned salaries 8 to

20 percent higher than the salaries assigned to the "before."

- **Greater cooperation from all constituencies.** People like working with you.
- **Self-assurance.** You recognize that you have a good image in place, and you're not insecurely monitoring yourself all the time.
- **Access to resources.** People help you get what you need to get the job done.
- **Nonproblematic relationships with "difficult" people.** Your image is oriented not to push any of the usual "hot buttons." that might provoke adverse reactions in your contacts.
- **Broader career options.** The right image can help people see you in any number of roles. You are not limited by your current job description.

CREATING YOUR IMAGE

The image you create for yourself depends on what you want. Maybe what you want is for the powers-that-be to perceive you as promotable. Maybe you want to be left alone to do your work. Or perhaps you want to be seen as a leader. What you want is how you should *appear.* That's the bottom line.

But your image must have substance. The days of an empty suit—or an empty skirt—are over. Image alone is not enough. Back in the 1950s and 1960s, many people could get away with merely looking the part. There were vice presidents who looked like vice presidents, and they could do well for themselves even if they weren't great leaders or had no special expertise. Today you're expected to present yourself well *and* have something unique to offer the marketplace. Both are essential. On the other hand, if you have plenty of substance but you don't have a suitable image, you probably won't go too far.

Image basically comes down to certain habits you can acquire.. Let's say Pete has good grooming habits, and his image is that of a man who takes care of himself. Another part of his image is his impeccable manners. In an age of boorish behavior, Pete stands out because he treats everyone with respect. Before he enters your office, he asks if it's a good time to see you; after he completes a transaction with you, he'll make sincere inquiries about your family. People like to have Pete around. Another of Pete's traits is that he sees the positive aspects of a problem. As a result, bosses can always count on him to raise the morale at a meeting.

Pete has cultivated a good image. You should too. Good grooming and etiquette are essential. But remember that image *isn't* a persona of the day or a flavor of the month. It won't work out in the office if you act like a team player today, but tomorrow you act like a creative genius who only works alone, and the next day you act like a leader. You can't put on an act; you have to develop a consistent demeanor and a series of behaviors that continually give off the right signals.

For example, suppose you want to be perceived as promotable. Every day you should:

Dress like those in the level above you. Don't dress well only when you have an official meeting with the boss. People see you every day. And it isn't simply your boss who decides whether you get promoted. Usually a number of other people also have input on such decisions.

Be helpful. Those who get promoted are seen to be genuinely interested in others' well-being. Few companies want to promote a narcissist.

Establish friendly relationships in other departments. Those connections may help you get a promotion and will certainly be useful to you after you are promoted.

Be energetic. People who get ahead always have an

extra tank of energy to switch over to. But you don't
want to seem *too* animated.

Be relaxed. Given the stress and downsizing in the
current job market, nobody wants a Chicken Little
running around screaming, "The sky is falling, the sky is
falling!" A relaxed persona will give your superiors
confidence in you.

Go the extra mile—whatever that mile is. Maybe the
boss, or the boss's boss, needs a report right away.
Volunteer to do it. You want a reputation for being
dependable and productive during crises.

Have a sense of humor. That shows you can detach
yourself emotionally from a situation and look at things
objectively. Keep your humor low-key, however. Belly
laughs are seldom appropriate in the workplace, unless
the boss leads the merriment. Smile instead.

Be eager to learn. Go for an advanced degree if the
organization encourages that. Often, simply being in an
MBA program gives you status and makes people see you
as a go-getter. (On the other hand, if the organization is
frenetic and always on the brink of chaos, it might not
look kindly on your spending time getting a degree for
yourself. But that doesn't mean you can't keep learning
more about the company's inner workings.)

Be enthusiastic. Companies *say* they want to hear your
reservations about a project, but they often really don't.
They might label you as negative. The workplace is not a
democracy, and freedom of speech should be used
cautiously.

These are just some of the habits you'll need to acquire if you
want to get ahead. You may acquire them slowly, through trial
and error. For example, if you want to be perceived as energetic, it might take time to get your rhythm right. If at first you
come across as overly animated, you will soon realize that, just

like an athlete, you have to pace yourself. If you want to be perceived as being just as energetic at 7:00 PM as you are at 9:00 AM, that means *not* indulging in a good, long yawn and *not* confiding in people how you can't wait to get home and go to sleep. Often the powers-that-be judge your energy level by how you handle yourself *after* official quitting time.

SYMBOLISM

The heartbeat of image is symbolism. That's because people see the world symbolically. As a boss or fellow employee, I don't always see Joe as Joe; I see Joe as a reliable worker. Image reduces people to manageable concepts that are easier to deal with. Image communicates to the world who you are—and the good news is, you can fine-tune the message.

Since I want to appear at the top of my game, I don't take copious notes during a meeting. If there's no one to take notes, I discreetly tape the meeting. Why? Because if the clients see me compulsively taking notes, I will lose points in their eyes. I won't look like an executive.

What do you want to be "seen as?" When you're considering your image, think about what every aspect of your behavior symbolizes—because that's how your colleagues and superiors will judge you. For example:

- You come in late frequently. Do people see that as laziness, disorganization, or a lack of interest in your work?
- You're often the last to leave the office at night. Do your colleagues see you as a good soldier, or do they perceive you as too inefficient to get your work done on time?
- You eat lunch with the bosses. Do your coworkers see this as a threat or just as smart business? If they see it as a threat, should you come up with a symbolic gesture—such as bringing in doughnuts on Friday—to demonstrate that you're still one of the gang? Or would that be perceived as condescending?

- You're studying for an MBA at night. Do your superiors see that as a waste of time or as a big help to the organization? Should you talk about your academic activities, or will that suggest that you're not fully focused on the job?
- The vice president publicly thanks you at a meeting. How do your colleagues interpret your reaction to the praise? Do they see you as single-mindedly ambitious, appropriately modest, or too self-effacing?
- You take off the day your dog dies. How would your colleagues and superiors perceive that decision? Would it be better for your image if you call in sick rather than revealing the real reason for your absence?
- You wear more expensive clothes than do most of your colleagues. Do they think you're "dressing for the level above you" and hence gunning for a promotion? Or do they simply see it as impeccable grooming?

It may be hard to answer these questions, because every workplace is different. But whether you work for Exxon Mobil or a small non-profit, the symbolic values that your image conveys, rightly or wrongly, can make all the difference in your future success.

THE TIME COMES

With so much change going on in the world of business, it's inevitable that at some point you might need to modify, or even overhaul, your image. How do you know when it's time? Here are some guideposts:

- You don't think your image is helping you to achieve the success you want. It helped you in the past, but it isn't helping with your present objectives.
- Someone has told you that you're handling yourself in a way that is self-defeating
- Your personal image no longer represents you. You've

outgrown it, and it's now misleading. (This can also be a problem with your online image.)
- You wish you had the courage to make changes in your image.
- You're in a crisis.

Changing an image can be difficult. We're not sure we can pull it off, and we don't know what reception our new persona will get in the office. But sometimes, such as in a crisis, it's necessary. Bart L. sensed that his laid-back image contributed to his getting laid off. So he sees Job Number One as creating a more energetic, responsive image.

The best approach in image change is to take it slowly and consider the image "reconfiguration" as an experiment that may or may not work. Build up new habits at a pace you can handle. That pace should be gradual enough that you can make midcourse corrections without people being aware of it.

Even with the right pacing, at some point people are going to notice your emerging new image, and they may comment. You have to be prepared to give them a logical explanation of why you're doing what you're doing. I wouldn't advise mentioning the word "image." That could open a whole can of worms. They might ask, "What was wrong with your old image?" "Why do you need a new image?" "Are you shooting for a promotion?" "Do you really think changing your image will help?" "What's so important about an image?"

There are myriad ways to explain why you're changing. You can say that you picked up some tips in a seminar, that your spouse made these suggestions, or that your mentor shared some recommendations with you. Or you can use your sense of humor to deflect their interest. For example, you can make light of your new "power" tie and explain that it was a gift. In short, there are countless ways you can satisfy the curiosity of coworkers and subordinates without violating your own sense of privacy.

If you try out aspects of a new image and sense they're not

working well, don't stay with them. Recreating an image is a tough job. You will probably make mistakes. Approach this the way an editor of a film would—that is, most of what you try will likely wind up on the cutting-room floor. Just sweep up the mess and keep working.

Things to Remember

- Everyone has an image, and that image should change with the times
- The right image can bring profound benefits
- Image is a series of habits you develop and integrate into your personality
- Image and image change require trial and error

9

HAVING INFLUENCE AT ANY LEVEL

This chapter is must reading IF:

* You believe in talent
* You feel powerless at work
* You're not able to sell your ideas
* Your job is threatened

If someone said you were influential, would you feel flattered or uneasy?

Probably a little of both.

THE GENERATIONS AND INFLUENCE

In my generation we'd be quite flattered. "Influential" signified a lot of positive things to us, ranging from knowing how to get things done to relating well to others.

But for your generation, "influential" might bring up images of your parents' era or suggest "manipulation." It's true, some people in positions of influence *are* manipulative, but true influence requires substance. You have to be able to offer something worthwhile in exchange for the other person's cooperation, ideas, or whatever.

You might also feel uncomfortable about influence because you don't want to get entangled in the web of obligations that having it involves. Instead, you say you'll get what you want purely on talent. After all, isn't this new economy a meritocracy? Shouldn't your talent win out over everything else? Well, from my experience, I've never seen talent alone win the day. There always has to be a sponsor or champion who will get the right people to notice those talents. That notice is frequently called the "big break." And you make the big break happen by connecting with a broad range of people—in other words, by creating a sphere of influence.

In this chapter, I'll discuss how you can increase your influence at work, even if you have an entry-level position. All of us have more influence than we think. There's no correlation between your rank in an organization and your degree of influence. Secretaries are often the most influential people in a company. An assistant manager I knew at an insurance company practically ran the department.

DEFINING "INFLUENCE"

What is "influence?" One of the best definitions I've come across was in a *Time* magazine cover story, *"The 25 Most Influential People in America."* According to *Time,* "Being influential is the reward of successful salesmanship, the validation of personal passion, the visible sign of individual merit."

INFLUENCE AND POWER

Influence is different from power. Power, as we've come to know it, usually emanates from position. Your bosses have power by virtue of the fact that they're the bosses; if a boss is demoted, that power disappears immediately. The minute a chief executive officer is no longer CEO, the power vanishes. There are exceptions: Edwin Artzt, former CEO of Procter & Gamble, became CEO of an Italian company after retiring. Another former Procter & Gamble CEO, John Smale, was able to work for three years supervising General Motors. But in general, power ends when the CEO job ends.

Anyone's power—even the CEO's power—can be taken away. The organization can fire you. It can demote you. But your *influence* is *yours*. You're the only one who can diminish or destroy your influence at work. You do that by compromising your credibility. I've seen many people screw up by over-promising—and then under-delivering.

Some people can have both power and influence. Former President Ronald Reagan was such a person. So was President John F. Kennedy. But President Clinton, according to *Time*, had only power, not influence. An article in *International Security* said the same of President George W. Bush. In the workplace, it's not enough to have power. To get things done, you also need influence. That's why there's so much office "politicking." That's how things get done.

One of the most brilliant practitioners of the art of influence was Jesus Christ. Though he had no worldly riches or outward power, he was able to persuade twelve men to leave their way of life and follow him. He used a variety of instruments ranging from eloquent speaking to performing miracles to persuade the public to embrace his point of view. Even in death, which his disciples described in memorable fashion, he continued to have profound influence.

THE MIND-SET FOR INFLUENCE

A WORLD OF ALLIES

Being influential starts with a mind-set. In *Influence Without Authority,* Allan Cohen and David Bradford point out that influence begins with a thinking pattern—specifically, with the belief that all those people at your workplace are potential allies. And Cohen and Bradford mean *all*. They suggest that you make even your boss an ally or strategic partner. I agree.

This mind-set is very different from how we usually see the world. Because we live in a competitive society, we tend to see the workplace as consisting of those we can run rings around and those who are clearly superior to us. We also tend to divide the workplace into friends and nonfriends. We wouldn't hesitate to call upon a friend for help, but we're standoffish with the nonfriends. Then there is a group at work we could call our allies. We know we can count on them for resources, but usually this isn't a large group.

This way of thinking eliminates a lot of people from being allies. However, it is possible to claim just about every person in your workplace as an ally. All it takes is a certain point of view. And that point of view is: *This person could be an ally down the road. I had better get to know this individual and what he or she is all about.* Your key ally could work in the mailroom or in the CEO's office. Resources come in all kinds of packages.

This ally, or partner, mind-set is the essence of influence. In "Negotiating to Shift Power Without Losing Influence," Leonard Marcus points out that influence comes from "new ways to frame and conduct the business of your institution." Walk into a meeting, and the traditional way of framing would be to divide the attendees into competitors, noncompetitors, friends, people we don't like, boss's friends, snitches, idiots, and flaming idiots. For you to reframe that collection of people as a roomful of potential allies is pretty radical, but it's the prerequisite of influence. Influential people in your organization have been doing it for years. They don't think, "Is this person nice"? They think, "Is this person a useful resource to me?"

START PLAYING

Another change you might have to make is in your willingness to participate in the dynamics of workplace influence. In a workshop a friend of mine attended, influence expert Jeffrey Pfeffer emphasized the importance of being in the game. "A lot of people at large companies," explains Pfeffer, "have the 'passover' rule." They think that if they keep their head down and blend in, nothing bad will happen to them.

Before there was a global economy, before downsizing and the Great Recession, it was possible to sit out the game in that way. No more. The global economy has made jobs precarious. Now you have to have influence to protect your job. That's what "air cover" is all about. Establishing "air cover" means that those in higher positions will protect you. Those who survive a layoff are usually those who are being protected; they got that protection through influence. Also, in a downsized world you're more visible and have more responsibility; to deal with that you need influence. You can't go to work anymore and assume you'll be okay if you just do your assigned tasks. If fact, you can't do many of today's new jobs at all without knowing how to tap into all sorts of resources. And that means being influential. "Influencing" has been written into your job description.

The third piece in the new mind-set means coming to terms with your values. Influencing is not a value-free activity. We all have codes of conduct for how we'll influence others. What's yours? What are you willing to do while influencing others, and what will you not do? For example, as Jeffrey Pfeffer observes in *Power: Why Some People Have It and Others Don't,* "Most people underestimate the effectiveness of flattery and therefore underutilize it." But maybe you're against the entire idea of flattery, and it feels manipulative rather than sincere to you. Well, those are your values, and you shouldn't go against them. But there are many other ways in which you can exert influence. There's no one technique you must embrace, but you must develop your own strategy.

INFLUENCE STRATEGIES

How do you learn to influence others? There are workshops, courses, and articles galore on the topic of influence strategies. But I would suggest that you begin by reading Robert Cialdini's *Influence: The Psychology of Persuasion.* As the title indicates, influence is really about getting someone else to agree with your point of view and to take the action you recommend. To be effective, teachers, ministers, politicians, change agents of every sort, and anyone in a leadership position must be influential.

In *Influence,* Cialdini introduces six principles of influence:

- **Reciprocity,** or the old give-and-take
- **Commitment and consistency,** or the human tendency to file new information in familiar grooves (or boxes) in the mind
- **Social proof,** or the power of what everybody is thinking (or seems to be thinking)
- **Liking,** or the tendency to deal with people you're attracted to
- **Authority,** or the deference we pay to the experts
- **Scarcity,** or the idea that potentially losing something makes the commodity more valuable

Let's look at those six and see how you can participate in the influence game.

RECIPROCITY

In my book *Power and Influence,* I call this the "favor bank." I like the image of a bank, because in reciprocity, just as in a bank, we're continually putting in and withdrawing favors. And as with a bank, if there are more withdrawals than deposits, you'd better find some fresh funds to deposit.

Reciprocity is perhaps the simplest strategy in influence. Just think back to those who've done favors for you at work. Maybe a coworker followed you to the dealership to have your car serviced, took you back to work, and later drove you back to the dealer to pick up your car. That's a big favor. How did you repay it? Or are you still repaying it? There is something hardwired in human nature that makes us want to reciprocate. Instinctively, we seem to know there is no free lunch.

In the favor bank you build up obligations or debts. Some debts you owe. Other debts people owe you. That sense of obligation underlies many transactions in the workplace. If Stan the accountant owes you a favor for helping his daughter get a job, then you can feel perfectly comfortable going to Stan and getting insider information about a company reorganization.

In his book, Cialdini discusses the power of reciprocity. He cites research showing that even a small favor—like bringing in a Coke for another person—imposes an obligation. The person who received the Coke feels compelled to reciprocate somehow. By giving out a free flower, the Hare Krishnas imposed an obligation, and the person who received the flower—the devotee refused to take it back—felt compelled to make a donation.

Every day at work, people have been imposing obligations on you, although you might not have realized it. You ask the boss on short notice for this Monday off, and she says yes. That's an obligation. So if she wants you to stay late one Friday night, you'll most likely comply. You owe her.

Since all the people you work with are potential allies, it will seem natural that you help them out. After all, you're on the same side. You share common ground. But make sure you get paid back. I know of one naïve woman who did a lot of favors and wasn't concerned about people paying her back. Her coworkers saw her as a loose cannon because she wasn't playing the reciprocity game according to the rules. The rules are clear. You play, you pay—and you get paid.

Many young people ask me: "Is it ever possible to have the brass in debt to you?" That answer is yes. You can have "accounts receivable" from top people in the organization. They need to get things done just like everyone else. An executive I knew was going through a rough time and couldn't concentrate on the speech he was working on with his speechwriter. The speechwriter took over a great deal of responsibility for preparing the speech, and the executive knew he was in debt for that. If you have accounts receivable in the executive wing, don't be shy about collecting. Executives got where they are because they understand this bartering system in an organization.

COMMITMENT AND CONSISTENCY

We all tend to stay in certain patterns. Maybe it's maintaining an aquarium filled with exotic fish. It would be difficult to abruptly change this pattern and start, say, collecting tropical birds instead. Our human craving for sameness, for familiarity, makes everything, including decision making, easier. When you give to charity, is it the same charity, such as for cancer or MS, or do you switch donations every year? I'll bet you rarely switch.

If you want to sell an idea or proposal to your coworkers, try to express it in the form of something they already know. For example, reengineering a company's resources could be introduced by comparing it to and contrasting it with Total Quality Management, a concept the employees are already familiar with. That helps ground the audience.

The smart boss who wants you to take graduate courses approaches you with what you already know: that the company has a tradition of intellectual excellence. Given that tradition, it seems a logical extension that you would be enthusiastic about taking one or two courses in your field. The boss can push the advisability of taking the second course once you're in the first course. The boss builds on your commitment.

Most people resist new ideas. That's why effective speakers make analogies to ideas with which the audience is already acquainted. Sports analogies are popular for a reason. They may be overused, but they really can be clarifying. Plus, they're reassuring. By using such a comparison, you can cast an unknown concept in a familiar light, which enables the listener to feel immediately at home with the new idea.

SOCIAL PROOF

What *everybody else* is doing influences what *we do.* Children know that. They let you know that *everyone else* in the fourth grade at St. Aloysius has already been to the Baseball Hall of Fame. Given that, how can you resist taking *your* child? The herd instinct is a powerful thing

If you want the boss to buy a certain type of software, cite all the other companies that are using it. If your subordinates don't like the summer schedule of working longer hours Monday through Thursday and a half day on Friday, mention the other organizations using this system. Point out that it's been in force at headquarters for two years and that most of the workforce has indicated in a survey how much they like the summer hours.

What's important is that you select your social proof from groups your coworkers or superiors respect. If you're at GE, and you tell your subordinates that a small company in Akron, Ohio, is already doing what they will be doing, it won't work. In an auto company years ago, a subordinate was resisting learning how to use a computer. The boss took her out to lunch and explained that everyone else in the department was already on board in terms of computers, and it was helping them enormously. Obviously, she was odd person out. That afternoon, she started to learn how to operate a computer. If you want to sell your daughter's Girl Scout cookies at work, tell your prospects that everyone else is buying, and cite the names of people or departments!

LIKING

When the academic market collapsed in the 1970s, mentors advised graduate students to get a job and then make sure "they like you." Even those in the highly cerebral corridors of academia recognized the power of being liked.

Yes, we live in a high-tech world, but that old-fashioned quality of being liked still has tremendous clout. People hire and promote those they like. One manager, after firing an underling, said to me, "I never liked her." That's how he summed up the whole relationship.

The truth is, we gravitate toward people who are similar to us. This brings us back to organizational culture. Go where you fit in. If you don't fit it, you're not going to be able to influence anyone. You'll be ignored. Or tormented.

If you think you need to become more likeable, take a sincere interest in other people. That means allowing what's happening in their world to become nearly as important to you as what's happening in yours. There's no way to feign this interest; if you try, your body language will give you away. Your sense of caring, says Daniel Goleman in *Emotional Intelligence,* must be real. And, if it's real, it will register in your body language. Goleman points out that 90 percent of communication of emotions is nonverbal. Many people in the office go through the motions of caring about you, but they're usually only busybodies—and everybody knows that.

AUTHORITY

I knew a clever woman with a baby boy and a difficult mother-in-law. The mother-in-law kept insisting that the baby was too old to be sucking his thumb. That wasn't true, but the woman reported to her mother-in-law that she had consulted a child therapist, who thought thumb-sucking at two years of age was okay. The woman got the results she wanted by citing an authority. The mother-in-law backed off.

Appealing to authority is a fundamental element of persuasion. You learn it in the first few days of Freshman Composition. You also learn that not all sources are equally authoritative. If you want your coworkers to come around to your way of thinking about the company's future, it wouldn't be all that convincing to cite the annual report or the organization's newsletter. What *would* get them to sit up and listen is for you to quote a few outside security analysts.

But this strategy has to be used with caution. If you *only* appeal to outside authority, you could come across as not having the self-assurance to have an opinion of your own. I vividly remember how in grad school one go-getter cited all sorts of authorities in a paper. The professor wrote, "But what do *you* think?"

SCARCITY

This is a strategy movie stars know well. So as not to be overexposed and, therefore, less valuable, famous actors will often limit the number of pictures they do. More isn't always better.

To become a prime influencer in your organization, move toward controlling the scarce resources in the organization. Let's say that the scarce resource is knowledge, and you and your team are an in-house think tank with a reputation for providing on-target information. That gives you tremendous influence. Everyone wants access to you, wants you to work on their projects, and wants you to present the information to customers.

Other scarce resources include time off, the fleet of company cars, capital for product development, access to the executive wing, and innovation the company will support. Whoever controls these has clout. Smart senators try to navigate their way to committee chairmanships that administer scarce resources, such as money.

You can even create your own scarcity. Your time, for example. If you're not always in your office or hanging around the water cooler, it's going to be more difficult for people to gain access to you. Being busy is a surefire strategy in influencing. Those in demand are not easily available. One of the great coups in influencing is for someone to have to leave a meeting early in order to get to another meeting.

But you don't want to become *too* scarce. Suppose your boss allowed you to work at home four days a week. Would that be a good idea politically? In some offices the more "face time" you put in, the more secure your position.

Things to Remember

- In the new economy, influence is a must
- Influence doesn't mean manipulation
- The world is full of allies
- Sitting out the game is not an option
- The key strategies are reciprocity, commitment and consistency, social proof, liking, authority, and scarcity

10

SCHOOL

This chapter is must reading IF:

- You're wondering if school is worth the time and money
- You're thinking about leaving or returning to school
- You sense that you need more training in your field

School—and plenty of it. Ever since the G. I. Bill sent veterans back to school after World War II, education has been perceived as an American right.

INTELLECTUAL CAPITAL

After high school came college. After college, it might have been graduate school for an advanced degree in math or medicine, and that was usually it. Now that we're in the Information Age, additional education is something to consider constantly. You struggle to decide: Should you go back to school part-time for a certificate in finance or a language-immersion course? Should you take a workshop about a new kind of software? Or should you invest in going back full-time in order to start a new career or significantly enhance the career you have?

You probably know some people who changed their lives by returning to school. Perhaps they were drifting in their jobs and careers. A hardworking, mid-level business employee, Eileen S. went back to school to get certified in teaching. As a high school teacher of business courses, she's happier—and gets the summers off. Adam D. went back to school to become a physician's assistant, and now he's working in a fancy hospital and making six figures. After college Jennifer M. realized that she hated her job in advertising and went back to school to study computer science. Now she is doing IT for a Fortune 500 company.

Higher education is the engine of the information economy. It helps supply the intellectual capital that "finances" the economy. Almost daily, I'm suggesting a course, seminar, or degree program to someone. I try to find the time to take courses myself.

Yet recently, to my amazement, higher education has come under attack. Many people have questioned the value of MBAs, law degrees, even the basic undergraduate BA. One organization—the Thiel Foundation —identifies a few exceptional students and offers them $100,000 to forget about college and pursue their ambitions on their own. I've heard talk of a "higher education bubble," and there is even a book called *College is for Suckers* by April Norhanian. Proponents of this view claim that getting a college degree is a waste of time that will improve neither your career prospects nor your lifetime earnings. I disagree—but I take their point. Thanks to the digital revolution, the economy is changing its shape. Plenty of jobs require skills that simply didn't exist twenty or thirty years ago, and degrees in certain traditional areas may no longer support your professional hopes.

So before you make a decision about where to go to school and what to study, make sure you know why you're doing it and what you hope to get out of it, especially if you're trying to advance your career. Do you want a stimulating job or a secure one? A fat paycheck? Lots of travel? A short commute? Ideally, you'll find all of the above. But often, you'll have to choose. For instance, accounting is a stable profession. The job prospects are excellent, and accountants can readily create their own small (or not-so-small) businesses. But April is always a crunch, and—let's face it—accounting can be tedious if you don't have the mind-set for it (though the best accountants I know don't seem to feel that way about it).

A career in journalism, on the other hand, can be incredibly exciting. It can literally take you all over the world, and, if you're talented, you will meet the most fascinating people on the planet. But as a journalism school graduate myself, it pains me to acknowledge that journalism, unlike accounting, is a rapidly shrinking field. Today, I'd think carefully before I wrote out that tuition check.

Then there are traditional fields, such as law, which until recently seemed about as solid as it can get. These days, competition for legal jobs is stiff, especially among recent graduates. Yet only a few years ago, earning a law degree practically guaranteed lucrative job offers. Applications to law schools shot up, and the schools responded, churning out so many graduates that eventually the supply of lawyers far exceeded the number of available positions. Legal jobs became scarce. In 2011, more than 43,000 people graduated from law school. Nine months later, only 55 percent of them had found a job working in law. On top of that, about 90 percent of law school graduates end up in debt to the tune of, on average, $98,500. So you have to ask yourself: Is law school worth that kind of investment? If you are passionate about the law, it is. But if going to law school is just something to do while you're waiting for a better idea to come along, there are other options. Before you enroll, you need to assess the pros and the cons of the specific program you're considering.

CALCULATING THE COSTS

First, there may be a personal cost. Going for a degree, particularly on the graduate or professional level, will demand an intensive commitment of time and energy. To succeed, you have to be single-minded. That "well-rounded" life you were encouraged to create usually gets put on hold. If you have a family, they could suffer. That may not be a price you want to pay. You also have to ask yourself: How will returning to school be perceived at work? If your boss has told you to get a master's degree in public health, you can feel free to go ahead and do so, even if it means taking a leave of absence. But if she has discouraged you from returning to school, then doing so could be a mistake, especially if you want to keep your job. When you return to the office, certificate in hand, you may find that the atmosphere has grown distinctly chillier than before. It's also possible that going for a degree will be so demanding that it could affect your performance on the job. At a petroleum company there was a man in public affairs who went to school at night for his law degree. During the day he was tired and irritable with coworkers, and that hurt his image more than his education helped it.

Second, getting an education doesn't necessarily pay off right away. You probably have friends with degrees from prestigious universities who are working as baristas or house painters or personal assistants. Maybe you've got a job like that yourself. Well, you're not alone. The sobering reality is that recent college graduates have a much tougher time finding a job than do more experienced workers. In 2011, more than 50 percent of college graduates under twenty-five were either unemployed or underemployed. In a restricted job market, a candidate fresh out of school with little or no experience is operating at a disadvantage.

Third, education can be expensive. In the academic year 2009–10, the average cost of an undergraduate education hovered around $21,000 a year. Graduate schools can be even pricier. Law schools charge more than $40,000 a year. Medical school tuition is about $46,000 a year. And at the top eighteen business schools, according to *Bloomberg BusinessWeek,* you will have to pay more than $100,000 for an MBA, a figure that does not include room, board, or books. In fact, if you attend Harvard Business School, the number one school on the list, you can expect to pay more than $168,000 for tuition and expenses. That's not nothing. It had better be worth it.

WEIGHING THE BENEFITS

Fortunately, most of the time, advanced education is worth it. It pays off on many levels, beginning with the most obvious: the intellectual. Education enriches the life of the mind. Does that sound self-indulgent or naïve? It shouldn't. Education introduces you to new concepts, new ways to understand the world, new ways to address problems, new sources of information. It deepens your knowledge, improves your powers of analysis, and stimulates your curiosity. The more you know, the more you want to know.

Second, education expands your network. With a little effort, you will be able to make friends and find mentors. This benefit, often overlooked, is not to be sneezed at. One young man, after working in a bookstore for three pleasant, aimless years, decided to get on a career path. He signed up for a couple of computer courses at an extension university. It wasn't a degree program (he already had a BA). It was only two courses. But he got to know one of his professors, and when he was ready to launch his job search, he asked her for advice. She gave him a name to contact. He followed through. As a direct result, he now oversees the website of one of our nation's most prestigious publications.

Third, advanced education generally bolsters the bottom line, although it's true that some professions have a rougher time than others. Recently, for example, architecture majors have struggled, as have those with degrees in the arts. Nonetheless, over a lifetime, people with more education are more employable, make more money, experience a higher level of job satisfaction, and enjoy greater job security.

Consider what happened in the financial crisis that began in 2007. By 2010, more than seven million jobs had been eliminated. Those layoffs affected people at every income level, but it did not affect them equally. According to the Georgetown Public Policy Institute, the overwhelming majority of the jobs that were lost—78 percent—required no education beyond high school. Jobs with higher educational requirements—anything from a few college courses to an advanced degree—were much less likely to be jettisoned. Moreover, when the economic crisis began to ease, those high-skill jobs were largely restored. Not so the low-skill, low-education jobs. They are still missing in action, and they're probably not coming back.

Finally, although there's no getting around the fact that education is expensive, you may not have to pay full fare for it, especially if you're working for an organization that will pick up some of the costs. Many organizations, including nonprofits, offer educational benefits. If your organization doesn't provide tuition reimbursement, you might start searching for one that does—because a company that values education enough to contribute to it is a company where you can grow.

The truth is that, despite a recent spate of bad publicity, education is still the smartest long-term investment you can make.

Stephen Greyser knows a lot about the intersection of business and education. An expert in marketing, corporate communications, the business of sports, and nonprofit management, he is the Richard P. Chapman Professor of Business Administration (Marketing/Communications) Emeritus at Harvard Business School. In addition to teaching, he has worked with businesses, nonprofits, arts organizations, and athletic organizations, including the Red Sox. He is still active in teaching and research.

Here's part of our conversation:

STEPHEN GREYSER

RLD: Several people I've spoken with recently have questioned the value of higher education. An article in *New York* magazine went further, stating that "The notion that a college degree is essentially worthless has become one of the year's most fashionable ideas." Why do you think that idea has arisen?

SG: I have no idea. And the main reason I have no idea is that it's a wrongheaded notion. However, one cannot overlook the fact that a few dropout entrepreneurs—people like Steve Jobs and Bill Gates—have managed very well without college degrees.

RLD: Those two men are extraordinary. They have abilities that the rest of us lack.

SG: That's why I would still say that for the vast majority of people who are seeking to advance themselves and develop their careers, having a college degree is virtually essential. But it is not sufficient. If you want to be a doctor, an MD, it isn't going to happen unless you have four years of college, done well, followed by medical school, followed by internships, residencies, et cetera. There's a lot of school to get to that career path. If your goal is to work in a service industry in the trenches and progress by dint of successful interpersonal relationships, maybe you don't need an advanced degree. I'm not saying it wouldn't be helpful; I'm saying that it may be less necessary.

RLD: I agree. It may be trendy to say that college doesn't matter—and maybe it doesn't for a few select individuals. For the rest of the world, a college degree is essential. But is it important to attend a top-tier college?

SG: I would say this: What is top tier for some people may not be top tier for someone else. Smaller campuses may be better for some people compared to large campuses. Or urban campuses may be better for some compared to suburban or even rural schools. A top-tier college as defined by the general population might be the right place for one person but not for another. And this is my key point—why let the rest of the world define what a good school is for you?

RLD: How important are internships for a student?

SG: For some fields they are highly important and maybe even essential, because they represent a way of finding out what working in a particular sector is like. Think about those people who might work as interns at the Dilenschneider Group. Interns are obviously not going to be developing strategic plans for important clients, but if the internship program is well shaped, they would have an opportunity to be part of a team, even if they're in the third row, and to understand what working with a client actually is like. So I think internships are really very helpful.

RLD: If a young person intends to go to graduate school—let's say for an MBA—is it smart to get real-world experience first?

SG: That is my view. And I hasten to say that that is the view of most of the leading business schools. My view is that working for a few years before graduate school, maybe even for more than a few years, has its merits. A lot of people complete college and still don't know what they want to do. Even a lot of people coming out of business schools still don't know what they want to do. But several years of work experience—to me, three, to others, two or five—can help. By working for a few years, you can gain maturity, you can gain knowledge, and particularly, you can gain a stronger sense of what your own goals might be.

RLD: Let's say you're going to work for three years between college and graduate school. Should you stick with one company, or is it okay to jump around a bit?

SG: I don't really know how business-school admissions officers look at job-hopping. Unless there is a compelling explanation for why a person moved from place X to place Y, I would think that showing what one can do in one environment has a lot of merit.

RLD: Is getting an MBA necessary for a person who wants a career in business?

SG: I think it's highly desirable. Remember, you don't advance because you decide it would be nice to be a boss; you advance because of your performance, and often your performance is based on knowledge, knowledge not only from books but knowledge of business situations combined with the ability to analyze them. That's why at Harvard Business School we believe in the case method as our core teaching vehicle. It puts young people into situations where they have to make decisions and defend them.

RLD: What do you think about going to law school or getting a PhD?

SG: If one wants to be a lawyer, one has to go to law school. Getting a PhD is not going to generate the financial value of a professional degree, because the fields one goes into afterward aren't necessarily deep-pocketed. People who have doctorates in education or divinity—where are the deep pockets there? They don't exist. Does that make those fields, or any of the liberal arts, any less satisfying to the individuals who enjoy them? Absolutely not. They are often every bit as satisfied as, maybe even more satisfied than, someone making more money in an unfulfilling career. Also, studying the liberal arts remains the best foundation for citizenship and for what I would call general knowledge for life. To my mind, advancing your education is not a question of assessing the financial value alone; it's a question of assessing the value to one's sense of self.

RLD: This gets at something you said in an address you gave a few years ago, the one you began by speaking Latin.

SG: Oh, you heard that.

RLD: I did. And I think you made that point very clearly: You start with knowing who you are.

SG: Exactly.

RLD: What education would you recommend to a young person who plans to enter advertising or public relations or any of the business-related fields you have expertise in?

SG: I think the most important thing is to understand what skills and knowledge areas are most germane in any given field. For example, if you are interested in corporate communications, understanding communications is important, whether through the lens of commercial communications or, better, through the lens of fields such as social psychology or cultural anthropology. These are the things to study in college. If you want to understand the power and influence of communications, start with psychology and perhaps even certain kinds of statistics. Understanding consumer behavior is another example. You don't learn it in a week, maybe you don't even learn it in a year, but it's important to understand it if you are trying to influence the behavior of particular groups. Obviously, getting an internship could also be a big help, because then you see firsthand how things are done. But first, you have to get basic knowledge.

RLD: What do you think about going back to school after graduation to take a course that's related to something you're doing now or might like to do in the future?

SG: I agree with that wholeheartedly. That's something that I would say is underplayed, especially in big-city areas where there are schools that offer extension courses. I can't imagine a person in New York City not wanting to take advantage of those programs, whether for degree purposes or not. I would also say this: If you're taking courses, know why you're doing it. Know what you think you need. And stay focused. I'll give you an example. Some people feel they need—and probably they do need—to have a more quantitative background. So, take a finance course, a quantitative methods course, or a management control course, managing with numbers. If you feel that that's going to give you a lift, then that's what you should do. Don't get distracted by taking other things because you—quote—think they'll be fun. There's nothing wrong with having fun, but it's more important to focus on the skills you're trying to gain.

RLD: Is there ever a point where you might take a course just for fun?

SG: Certainly. When it's not a career-advancement decision. You can eventually get to a stage where you shift from taking courses for skill development to doing so for personal enjoyment. That can easily happen if you're in a geographical location that allows you to go to schools where they have good faculty teaching in the evening. So you look at the catalog. Maybe you always wanted to learn more about Shakespeare, but you didn't want to digress, so you never took a class. But at a certain point you might say, maybe I'll take a course one evening a week. It's a personal-satisfaction decision.

RLD: So as a younger person, you might take that quantitative management course. As an older person, you can take art history or guitar or whatever you want.

SG: Exactly.

RLD: Which areas of study look the most promising to you in terms of employment?

SG: I would say the most promising is in the realm of technology, and if you can combine technology with business administration, that's pretty powerful.

RLD: Is there ever a situation where it's a mistake to go back to school?

SG: I'd say it could be a mistake at a particular time but not necessarily at another time. For example, if someone is struggling with difficult family circumstances or serious financial need, seeking more education might just add to the burden, financially as well as time-wise.

RLD: Can you describe a really satisfying educational experience that you've had?

SG: I'll give you two. I went to high school at America's first

school, Boston Latin School, founded in 1635, before
Harvard. I was there for six years, starting in seventh
grade, which we called Class Six. It was a satisfying and
rewarding (albeit difficult) educational experience, the
most important preparation for life that I ever had—
more important than Harvard, more important than
Harvard Business School. Now, that doesn't mean that
those others weren't important; it just means that I built
my foundation in the discipline of study and of understanding the world in those six years at Boston Latin.
The most satisfying education *career* experience I've had
is teaching at the Harvard Business School. You may or
may not have noticed a sentence in my bio that reads,
"Known as 'the Cal Ripken of HBS,' he has never missed
a class in more than 40 years of teaching." I consider that
an important part of what, in today's world, would be
called my own personal brand (although I don't think of
it that way), because my students gave me that designa-
tion many years ago, and it's stuck. They said, "Professor,
Cal Ripken has gone over two thousand games without
missing a single one, and you're doing the same thing
here, so we're going to call you the Cal Ripken of the
Harvard Business School." I'm proud of that because,
even though I've done many other things, I always remember what gave me my admission ticket and allowed
me to do a lot of the things that I did, and that was consistently showing up and doing the job well.

RLD: I have a final question that you can probably answer with
a single word. Do you prefer to be called professor or
doctor?

SG: I try to avoid being called doctor, because I believe that
"doctor" should be reserved for people with medical
degrees. So I am called professor, which I consider appropriate, especially when I'm being introduced in a
professional context. The title signals students, clients,
and colleagues that I have an advanced degree and am

considered an expert in my field because I have knowledge

RLD: That's what matters. You can network all you want and never miss a meeting, but if you don't have the knowledge, you're cooked. Knowledge is power.

SG: Exactly.

TAKING CONTROL

I can tell you from my own experience in college and graduate school that, to make your investment pay off, you have to gain control over the educational process. You shouldn't just go to class every day and think you're getting an education. You have to be proactive about your personal and professional development.

How can you take control?

The answer goes back to self-knowledge. Before you embark on a demanding educational program, you have to know who you are and what you want from school. For instance, if you're thinking about getting an advanced degree but are unsure whether you'll have the time or the interest, then try it one course at a time. Put one toe into the water first.

Also, do your homework—before you enroll. If you're contemplating getting a master's degree in field X or Y, go to practitioners in that field and ask them candidly what a graduate degree will get you in the work world. It may not be necessary or even helpful. Find out before you commit yourself.

Once you're enrolled in school, whether full-time or part-time, take full advantage of campus life. Keep an eye on upcoming events, and when a guest speaker is addressing a topic that interests you, go to the lecture. Attending lectures, something I do on a regular basis, is an easy way to keep up with new thinking and simultaneously do a little networking.

More important, participate in class and get to know your professors. They can mentor you. They can introduce you to people. And they can write glowing letters of recommendation—but only if they know who you are. Be sure to cultivate them.

Similarly, befriend your fellow students. One evening business program had wine-and-cheese parties to encourage students to network. Those get-togethers proved as important to their careers as understanding a balance sheet. Strong bonds are made in educational programs. You should make time to connect.

Finally, don't retreat completely into student life, tempting though it may be. Stay in touch with practitioners in the field outside the university. If you're working, make sure your education doesn't interfere with your job performance. And never get so engrossed in your studies that you lose touch with the outside world.

Things to Remember

- Higher education is the engine of the Information Age
- Higher education is an expensive investment, both in money and time
- You have to be proactive in getting an education

11

YOUR WORK AND
YOUR PERSONAL LIFE

This chapter is must reading IF:

- You want more in your life than just work
- You're ambitious and worry that taking advantage of flextime programs can hurt your career
- You wonder why organizations have begun to help employees balance their work and personal lives
- Your parents were 100 percent dedicated to the organization but ended up feeling betrayed, and you don't want to repeat their mistakes

You've probably heard that some organizations help employees balance work and personal life through family-friendly policies such as flexible scheduling (flextime), job sharing, telecommuting, subsidized child care, tuition reimbursement, and paid maternity, paternity, and adoption leave.

You probably have some questions about those policies. For example, you might be wondering:

- Does all this flexibility come penalty-free? Suppose your boss allows you to leave at 4:45 PM instead of 5:00 to pick up your infant daughter at day care. Will your boss hold this

against you when it comes to bonuses and promotions? And if that happens, is there anything you can do about it?
- Your parents used to talk about how rigid corporations were. It really was a nine-to-five world. Why are business organizations changing? Is it in their self-interest to help employees balance their lives?
- Your spouse expects you to do chores around the house. Yet you work long hours, and you're thinking of going to law school at night. Can those family-friendly programs help you out?

Sheila Wellington, executive-in-residence at New York University's Leonard N. Stern School of Business, is acutely aware of these issues. For ten years, she was president of Catalyst, a nonprofit focusing on women in the workplace. Before that, while raising her sons, she was vice president and secretary of Yale University. She is also the author of *Be Your Own Mentor.* Here's part of our conversation about work/life balance:

INTERVIEW: SHEILA WELLINGTON

RLD: You and I first spoke about work/life balance about fifteen years ago, when I asked what you thought this issue would look like in the future. Let me read you something you said then.

SW: Oh, dear! What did I say?

RLD: You were optimistic. You pointed out that women were entering the workforce in unprecedented numbers and that work/life balance mattered to everyone. Then you said—and I quote—"There will be more programs at more businesses, and those programs in place at that time will have more depth, more options, and be more widely used by employees . . . That's because organizations are finding out that flexible programs reduce turnover and make it easier to recruit and retain both women and men." We're well into the twenty-first century now. Was your prediction accurate?

SW: I don't truly think that that prediction has come to pass as a general proposition. The outstanding companies fifteen years ago are probably still outstanding, and the business case for this issue is as powerful as ever. But the kind of massive change that I seemed to expect has not taken place. I now teach at NYU Stern Business School, and I must say that work/life balance remains an issue that especially troubles women students.

RLD: And yet surely we've seen improvements.

SW: Well, men are more aware of the complicated nature of the issue. There's more child-care leave for fathers, and that's welcome. Also, in terms of women's experience in the workplace, there have been many more sexual-harassment cases won, and there has been a shift in culture in terms of sexual harassment. That's an area where there's been progress. We've also seen some change on the public front. In 2008 there was a woman in contention for a presidential nomination and another running for vice president. That was a triumph. The fact that Hillary Clinton was an extraordinary secretary of state has been a triumph, and there have been significant breakthroughs in terms of Supreme Court justices. These are splendid things, but we are talking here about exceptions. We're not talking about major shifts for women.

RLD: What about within the business world?

SW: I'm sorry to be pessimistic in my analysis, but it's backed up by data. For every Sheryl Sandburg, virtually the same number of women as there would have been fifteen years ago are stuck in the pipeline. And the persistence of the wage gap between low-pay and medium-pay jobs is as strong as it was. Fifteen years ago, there was stuff coming out predicting all kinds of change. And yet, here

we are. Some companies are excellent at promoting gender equality, but there has not been a massive breakthrough. Look at law firms. Beginning in the early 1980s,
women started to make up more than 40 percent of the
classes in the top twenty law schools—but we have not
seen significant gains in female partners. The number of
women partners is stuck below 20 percent. So something's going on.

RLD: What do you see at the business school?

SW: Women make up a very healthy percentage in business
school, but the overall data are absolutely the same. There
has been a little bit of an uptick in the number of women
corporate officers, but these are in staff roles—in public
relations, in external relations, in human resources—and I
don't think there's been a dramatic change on other
fronts.

RLD: So the CEO and the CFO are still male.

SW: That's right. It's pretty stagnant, and it's certainly not
what many of us in this field hoped for and, indeed, even
expected. Work/family is still a major issue. In academia,
people point frequently to the number of women college
and university presidents, but the tenure data has barely
moved. I've investigated it, and it's the same story. I'm
not totally discouraged, but I think it's going to take another fifteen years and an even greater push on all fronts.

RLD: Has public policy helped?

SW: The FMLA, the Family and Medical Leave Act, hasn't
made the kind of profound impact that one would expect. So there we are.

RLD: Given all that, what do you tell students who are entering the market?

SW: I give them a lot of advice about getting a job and how
to evaluate it. Unfortunately, these days, the focus has to
be on securing a job. For the individual who is just grad-
uating, the game is "Get a Job."

RLD: What kind of benefits should young people look for?

SW: For women, the first step they should take is to ignore the stock speech about how dedicated the organization is to gender equality and look instead at the numbers. Look for the achievement record, not just a line of baloney. How many women officers are there, and what slots are they in? How many women are on the board or the executive committee? The immediate job data are beside the point. Look at the data on people who've been around for seven, ten years, and see what their future looks like it holds. Hiring may be fine, but that's not where you want to focus. You want to focus on where people have been after seven to ten years. Look at the numbers. Then look at what programs are offered, and look at the utilization of those programs. If somebody says there's a family-leave or flexible time program, well, that's good, but the mere existence of such programs is only a marginal aid to insight. The issue is not only the availability of the programs; it's their utilization and the impact of using them. There is still a pervasive idea that because a woman—or a man, for that matter—makes use of these programs, it's a sign of reduced commitment. Sometimes benefits such as extended maternity or paternity leave are technically on the books, but if you actually take them, it slows your career down.

RLD: Does the slow pace of progress cause you to feel discouraged about these issues?

SW: I'm an optimistic, cheerful person, but I think it's going to take another fifteen years and a greater push on all fronts—public policy as well as business policy. I should add that things seem to be picking up, at least in the rhetoric. But we will have to see if this wave of conversation has a greater impact than it has in the past.

THE "ORGANIZATION MAN"

The world of work that exists today is very different from the world I entered in the 1960s. One difference is that a generation or two ago most women didn't remain in the workforce after marriage. And men had very little choice in how we handled our lives—both work and personal.

The choices or flexibility many of you now have in the workplace are relatively new. From the end of World War II until the 1980s, when computers became ubiquitous, there was an "Organization Man" mentality in America. Men went to work in large organizations. That's where the opportunities were. In return for access to those opportunities, the men conformed to the dictates of the organization. That might have meant wearing a hat to work. It might have meant not leaving the office in the evening until the boss left. It might have meant living in the suburb the organization wanted you to live in.

The Organization Men sacrificed just about everything to the job. If that meant working fourteen hours a day and missing their children's birthday parties, they did that. Although they might have been bone tired, they still were willing to go for drinks with colleagues after work, if that's what the organization expected. If there was a rush project, their families might not see them for weeks. In return for this intense loyalty to the organization, they were relatively well paid and had a shot at perks and promotions.

In his famous book *The Organization Man,* William Whyte Jr. said that in the world of the Organization Man, "work . . . is dominant. Everything else is subordinate . . . Whatever the segment of it [his life]—leisure, home, friends—he instinctively measures it in terms of how well it meshes with his work."

I was an Organization Man for years. Believe it or not, it had its good points. Being part of a large, well-known organization gave me an identity. And there was no ambiguity—the rules were clear. It never dawned on me to question those rules or to ask for a few months off to climb a mountain. My boss would have doubted my commitment—and my sanity. But as the economy, society, and I changed, being an Organization Man became an increasingly bad fit for me. And I was not alone. Everywhere, a growing number of men are demanding more balance in their lives. And so are working women.

THE POST–ORGANIZATION MAN'S WORLD

Because of those changes, the Organization Man is becoming a dinosaur. New policies have emerged, beginning with the Family and Medical Leave Act, which President Clinton signed in 1993. It states that employees are supposed to get up to twelve penalty-free, unpaid weeks off for the birth or adoption of a child, to care for a seriously ill family member, or to recover from a serious illness. While these benefits may not always accrue in reality—progress sometimes takes a while—their presence augurs well. In addition:

- According to research conducted in 2012 by the Society of Human Resources Management (SHRM), 61 percent of the organizations surveyed offered wellness programs, and 45 percent provided health and lifestyle coaching.
- A 2010 government survey of employers found that over half offered flexible arrangements to some (but not all) employees. Another survey, this one of workers, indicated that under a third of full-time employees enjoyed flexible hours. Either way, this is a perk the Organization Man could not have imagined. Trust me; when I began my career, flexible hours of any sort were a fantasy.
- In 2012, nearly a third of the one hundred most desirable companies to work for (Google earned the top spot) provided on-site child care.
- And here's a statistic that is nothing less than astonishing: In 2011, an analysis by SHRM found that a full 28 percent of the companies surveyed provided a lactation room for nursing mothers. Times have definitely changed.

There are a number of factors driving this revolution in the workplace. One factor is the change in the nature of work. With global competition, employees are expected to be more productive, creative, and accountable. Usually that entails putting in more hours. More hours also mean more stress. Employees have to learn to deal with that. Also, spending more hours at work means there's no one at home to let in the plumber.

That was not a problem when I was growing up. In 1950, most women were not employed outside the home. Only 34 percent worked. By contrast, in 2010, according to the US Department of Labor, more than 58 percent of all women over sixteen were either working or looking for work, and the labor force was 47 percent women. That number is expected to grow. A Gallup poll conducted in 2012 found that even among women with children under eighteen, the vast majority—about 63 percent—work. The dual-career household has become standard, and in addition there has been a sizeable increase in the number of single-parent families. So who lets in the plumber or takes the child to the after-school dental appointment or soccer game? The answer is not so clear.

These new realities are not easy to deal with for anyone. Employees are partly looking to employers for answers, and many employers have tried to provide them. For example, SAS, which topped a *Forbes* Magazine list of the best companies for work/life balance, offers telecommuting, job-sharing, flexible Fridays between Memorial Day and Labor Day, sabbaticals, an adoption mentoring program, elder-care assistance, and more. The new mind-set is that both the organization and the employee are supposed to pitch in and find solutions.

There is also a change of consciousness about work. With downsizing and consolidation eliminating so many jobs, people are more hesitant to make work "everything." Many in the current workforce feel betrayed by their companies' lack of commitment to them. They made tremendous sacrifices on behalf of their employers and still wound up losing a job or a number of jobs, and it is often difficult to find comparable jobs. Increasingly work is seen as a means to support a lifestyle—not as an end in itself.

Many initiatives to help employees balance work and family are inexpensive or free, and offering them is a smart thing for an organization to do. They help employees and provide the organization with a progressive image. These initiatives can include seminars on stress, sharing jobs, flextime, and working from home.

Many organizations that have offered work/personal-life benefits have had excellent results. One result is good public relations. When a company is willing to acknowledge that, yes, you have a life, it makes it easier for them to recruit and retain talented people. That's why, when *Forbes* and *Fortune* publish their annual lists of the hundred best companies to work for, people take notice. Offering desirable perks and flexible programs is now a factor in helping organizations develop positive images.

Work/life benefits are also a clear signal to employees that the organization cares. This is a much-needed signal at a time when organizations can no longer offer lifetime employment yet are still asking for outstanding performance.

Turnover, which is expensive, is frequently reduced. For example, after the insurance company Aetna introduced family-friendly policies, 91 percent of new mothers returned to work versus 70 percent before the benefits were offered. That saved Aetna $2 million. First Tennessee Bank established a policy allowing full-time employees to become part-time employees and keep their benefits. About 85 percent of full-timers who were considering quitting for personal reasons stayed with the organization.

When companies make it possible for employees to balance their personal concerns with their professional goals, they reap immense rewards in terms of productivity, satisfaction, and loyalty.

And from what I've observed, generous work/life policies

help strengthen some of the bonds that exist between employers and employees. You might say that these policies are part of their new social contract. When bosses let you work from home, saving you a two-hour commute, you're going to feel well-disposed toward them.

THE PITFALLS

Sadly, some organizations have not kept their policies current with the new economic, social, and legal realities. Especially in a distressed economy, some companies find it challenging to focus on anything other than the bottom line. When that happens, work/life benefits may suffer.

One reason some organizations find it difficult to address those issues is that doing so requires a change of attitude. A tremendous one. Employers must move from a point of view that employees need to be be carefully supervised to one that allows employees to supervise many aspects of their own work, including how they use their time.

You, too, must change your mind-set. You have to be clear about what you want from your career. You can no longer drift. If you want to be a vice president by the time you're thirty—and it's possible—it might not be wise to switch from full-time to part-time work. Working part-time may enhance your personal life, but it could also put the brakes on your ascent in the organization. There are always trade-offs.

For example, flextime and telecommuting let you determine your own schedule. But when you're working from home, you're not participating in office life in the same way. You're less visible. That's a trade-off you might not want to make.

Another pitfall of work-life balance policies is the possible repercussions. Organizations never were and never will be perfect institutions, and there is considerable variation in how these policies are approached at different organizations or even in different departments of the same organization. For instance, one organization might have family-friendly policies on the books, but you will find that you are penalized if you use them. We probably all know stories about women who took advantage of their company's maternity leave. When they returned, they were no longer on the fast track. The "Mommy Track" is a problem that has yet to be solved.

Perhaps your organization is enlightened about helping employees balance their lives, but it's a different story with your particular boss. He says you can work at home, but the next time you're back in the office, he's abusive toward you. You get the message—and no longer work at home. Or you and your boss may be happy as clams with you working three days a week at home. However, your competition for a promotion has the ear of the boss all day, every day—and a chance to eat lunch with him those three days you spend at home. You have to take charge of your career and use common sense in evaluating the risks that accompany flexibility. Check out how employees who have used policies you are interested in are faring. Were any sidelined? Every organizational culture is different, but in some cases, the smart move may be to avoid these policies or to postpone your use of them until you're solidly established.

For instance, if you want to become a partner in a law firm, you might work full-time until you achieve that status and then a few years later request a less arduous schedule. In the new world of work, many things are negotiable that weren't negotiable just a decade ago. But every case is different. Just because Jim became partner and then cut back to thirty hours a week doesn't necessarily mean that you can do likewise. Jim may bring in $50 million of new business a year. Because he's a rainmaker, he gets special treatment.

Lesson number one on the balance issue: If you're applying for a job, take the time to find out what the real scoop is about the balance of work and personal life. If you're assigned to a new department or new boss, use networking to find out their positions on balancing work and personal life. Not all organizations, departments, or individuals realize how much this issue matters to potential employees.

On the other hand, maybe this issue means very little to you. Maybe it'll never mean much. Then you don't have to rule out organizations that aren't helping employees juggle their busy lives. Your career decisions are yours. Unlike in the days of the Organization Man, there is no longer a single model for success.

Things to Remember

- It's in an organization's self-interest to help employees balance work and personal life
- You, too, have to be flexible, not just the organization
- Not every organization is family-friendly
- Evaluate the possible ramifications of using these work/life policies
- This may not be an issue you're concerned about yet—or ever. You can now configure your career in an almost infinite number of ways

12

THE RIGHT THING TO DO

This chapter is must reading IF:

- You want to become more manners-literate
- You don't feel comfortable at professional lunches and other professional social functions
- You've offended a number of people
- You envy how self-assured some people are in your office
- You were a latchkey kid, and no one seemed to have time to explain the social graces to you

Was the father of our country, George Washington, so successful because he was a brilliant strategist or, as *US News & World Report* says, because he had good manners? Probably a bit of both.

WHY HAVE GOOD MANNERS?

One immediate benefit of becoming more manners-literate is that you immediately become more sure of yourself. Old-money WASPs, who've almost always had excellent manners, have also almost always handled themselves with great self-assurance.

THE COMPETITIVE EDGE

Good manners have always been a way for up-and-comers to differentiate themselves from their competitors.

Two young men came to interview for a job at my firm recently. One had good manners. He acted like a guest and didn't get too comfortable. He said "please" and "thank you." And he demonstrated, by listening carefully, that he valued the time I was spending with him. The other young man seemed to be "above" manners. He slouched. He was a little too forward. He demanded, not requested, information from me. He got a little too comfy too fast. If I offer either one of them a job, it'll be the young man with manners. The other turned me off.

Good manners have helped me throughout my career. For example, one way I set myself apart from the competition is by hosting dinner parties for our key clients and prospects at my home. Doing this requires a lot of know-how in the social graces, even for my two sons. My family and I are able to make an impression on the guests by practicing the laws of hospitality, laws that go back to the Middle Ages, laws that make guests feel welcome and special. On one occasion, before a Japanese guest came over, I taught my son Geoffrey how to bow. Geoffrey practiced for days and was eager to do his thing. Well, my Japanese friend was so pleased by this gesture that he took the time to show Geoffrey how to improve his bow. The visit was a great success.

Right now, if you have good manners—even just so-so ones—you're ahead of the game. That's because, since the 1960s, many people have ignored the social graces. They don't know that they should walk their guest to the door or send a thank-you note—not an e-mail. Technology, for all its benefits, has introduced new forms of rudeness. In competing for new accounts, I can run rings around firms that are rough around the edges. Their rough spots say: *We don't know what we're doing. And because we don't, we're nervous.* As a result, people don't feel at ease around them. People love the self-assured. Self-assurance says: *I'm in control, and therefore I can help you.* My manners help clients have confidence in me.

THE BOTTOM LINE

Good manners not only get you in the door, they help an organization's bottom line. That's because good manners reflect both respect for others and the wish to make them feel comfortable. As Miss Manners (a.k.a. Judith Martin) has pointed out in *Fortune,* if workers are not treating one another with respect, then you have to wonder how they're treating customers. Miss Manners is right. That's why organizations are hiring "etiquette consultants" to do everything from training the customer-service staff to educating employees in the new workplace mores. For instance, should you give a shower for a pregnant secretary who isn't married? Is it inappropriate to read faxes coming in for others? And when is it okay to forward an e-mail?

A whole cottage industry has sprung up to take care of those matters of etiquette. There are newspaper and magazine columns, websites, podcasts, blogs, and thick books on the subject by Miss Manners and others. There are corporate consultants such as Telephone Doctor Nancy Friedman, who teaches phone etiquette, and Jacqueline Whitmore, whose clients range from the Department of Defense to Bloomingdale's. If you are looking for an entrepreneurial activity, this is a growing field.

BONDING

Have you ever had a manager or client who treated you with respect and made sure you felt comfortable? Didn't that immediately establish a bond? I go the distance for those who treat me well. On the other hand, I ignore those who treat me poorly. No need to get even; the big world out there will chew them up and spit them out.

The world is unforgiving to the unmannerly. People have long memories for when they've been treated rudely. The head of Windows at Microsoft found that out when, instead of making a presentation, like everyone else, at a senior-executive retreat, he told his colleagues to read his blog and then left before they made their presentations. He was canned. I wonder if New York Yankees owner George Steinbrenner would have had a less volatile career if he had had good manners. An executive at a cosmetics company who was hosting a meeting of executives from around the country, including me, alienated us all with a public temper tantrum. Because he was unhappy about how the food services had set up the room, he yanked the tablecloth and literally sent everything flying. It was a bad way to start off relationships.

HOW ARE YOUR MANNERS?

It's probably true that the manners of every generation inevitably dismay the previous generation. The Baby Boomers, who came of age in the freewheeling 1960s and 1970s, famously horrified their elders—and something similar goes on today. Your generation of digital natives sees nothing wrong, for instance, with sending a wedding invitation via e-mail. (Don't be surprised if Grandma objects.) And I'm sure you have noticed that talking on your cell phone in public can drive older people crazy. With every advance in communication, habits and expectations change. New rules of etiquette will eventually develop and be widely understood. Until then, misunderstandings and faux pas are all too easy to stumble into.

We are also facing another etiquette challenge: a widespread loss of civility. You can see it in politics, on reality TV, and on the Internet, where crude and insulting comments abound. That climate makes it difficult to know what is acceptable and what is not. Yet rude behavior, even if rudeness is not the intent, can destroy a career. Fortunately, the rules of courtesy are not hard to master.

BECOMING MANNERS-LITERATE

THE GOLDEN RULE

All manners are based on the Golden Rule. You treat others the way you want to be treated. Suppose you would like job interviewers to let you get comfortable with them before they ask the "hard" questions, such as why you lost your last job. Well, that's exactly how you should treat those you interview at your office. Manners are not just a set of arbitrary rules that some expert made up; they are meant to create a uniform, understandable social protocol that makes life easier for everyone.

Manners may seem like rigid rules, though, when they pertain to something you have not experienced. For example, most etiquette books now have sections on how to do business overseas. They'll tell you that in some Arab countries it is bad manners to expose the bottom of your shoe, and that in Japan you don't want to be the first to drink tea. If you haven't traveled internationally on business, all that may seem silly or as dry as dust to you.

But when you follow the suggestions in the etiquette guides, you make your counterparts in the other country feel comfortable. And that's exactly how a well-mannered person wants to make another person feel. Any awkwardness puts your host in an uncomfortable position. If you don't bring your host in Japan a gift, for instance, that person will feel baffled, because normal business protocol has been violated. That will create distance between the two of you. You don't want any unnecessary barriers getting in the way of the relationship.

In a Dale Carnegie seminar, students were asked not to use foul language. One lover of four-letter words buttonholed the instructor and said, "What are you guys, prudes?" The instructor explained that bad language isn't recommended because it will offend many people. A well-mannered person doesn't want to offend *anyone*. A well-mannered person wants to be sensitive to other people's feelings—and most people aren't comfortable with four-letter words.

Think back to your last job interview. Did the interviewer demonstrate bad manners by lighting a cigarette without your permission or asking you your age (which is also illegal)? If so, you probably felt uncomfortable, which means that you probably didn't perform as well as you could have. But skillful interviewers at reputable organizations, such as Procter & Gamble, have impeccable manners. That helps you soar when you present yourself for a job.

YOUR VALUES

Manners begin with your values. Would you help a colleague meet a deadline if he came into work after a night on the town at 11:00 AM? I don't know about you, but for me this situation—one in which the person brought trouble upon himself—wouldn't flash brightly on my compassion screen. I'd ignore the guy.

Or perhaps your acquaintance down the hall is having trouble meeting a deadline because her boss suddenly died. She's been trying to get help through official channels, but with reengineering, everyone is overloaded. Would it be good manners to help her out as much as you can? Is that something you'd like someone to do for you? If it is, then it's good manners to help that person.

Do you believe that it's good manners to really listen when someone is talking to you? Then you'll listen, no matter what else is going on in your head. *Not* listening is the *height* of bad manners, at least in my book.

Manners are not arbitrary. They are closed linked to values. To assess your own manners, list your values. Then put an example of how that value influences your manners, like this:

I'm compassionate. Therefore, I would feel sorry for someone who has no way to pick up his car at the service center. So I consider it good manners to give this person a ride if he asks for my help.

I'm competitive. Although I'm on a team, I still think that it's within the boundaries of good manners to call attention to my own achievements, as long as I do it in a way that doesn't detract from the accomplishments of the other players. I might send a memo to my boss pointing out what parts of the strategy were my ideas. I'd attach documentation, such as memos I sent the team about those ideas.

Incidentally, in *Executive Etiquette in the New Workplace*, Marjabelle Young Stewart finds no breach of etiquette in team players differentiating themselves from the other players. Stewart says that when your interests don't coincide with the interests of the team, "it is important to know how to look out for yourself while maintaining a veneer of good manners." Your goal is to position yourself as a team player while you gracefully promote yourself.

I have a soft spot for the disabled because my brother is disabled. In dealing with disabled people, I'll make sure they aren't ignored.

In *The Complete Business Etiquette Handbook,* Barbara Pachter and Marjorie Brody point out that it is good manners not to ignore the disabled. In addition, a well-mannered person will not use certain words with the disabled—such as "crippled" or "handicapped"—and will accommodate the disability. For example, when talking to someone who is hard of hearing, well-mannered people speak clearly, stand close, and make sure the other person can see their lips.

Take the time to examine your values. The best foundation for your manners is your own code of values. People will be able to identify you as an individual based on that code. That is one way you can differentiate yourself from others. Good manners, especially in these days of incivility, make you memorable.

RESEARCH

Your next step in becoming more manners-literate is to research the topic. Every library and every major bookstore has a section reserved for etiquette. On the shelves you will find books that range from *Business Etiquette for Dummies* by Sue Fox to *Emily Post's Etiquette, 18th Edition,* a 700-page tome written by the great-great-grandchildren of the manners maven. Just like a standard medical reference, one of those etiquette books should be on your shelf at home and in the office.

When you first pick up one of these books, it may seem like a formidable read. Wrong. The information, I've found, is fascinating. There are so many aspects of human relationships that I'd never thought about in terms of manners. For example, how can you register a complaint without alienating your boss? Or, how is the boss supposed to treat a secret office romance (that everyone knows about)? These books provide common-sense answers.

You can also do research electronically. That's most useful when you want advice about something specific. For example, maybe you have questions about holiday gift giving. To whom do you have to give a present? What gifts imply disrespect? Google "office gift-giving" and add "Forbes" or "Fast Company" or "Wall Street Journal." You will find all the advice you need.

Other electronic resources include the Etiquette Daily Q&A Blog of the Emily Post Institute (www.etiquettedaily.com). How should you deal with a colleague's overpowering perfume? How should you handle office solicitations? This blog tells all.

Another way to do research is the oldest in the world: Ask someone's opinion. Suppose you share a secretary with eight other people. Over the past twelve months, she only typed up one eight-page report for you. Should you give her a going-away gift? This is something you can talk over with someone who understands the politics and manners of the office. And when you make a decision, it's best to err on the side of being generous.

THE NEW INCIVILITY IN BUSINESS

When you were applying for jobs recently, were you ticked off that some employers didn't even acknowledge your follow-up letter or inform you that the job was filled? Join the club. The professional world used to be known for its impeccable manners. If you applied for a job, you would hear from the employer promptly. And if you didn't get the job, they would send you a personalized letter of regret. No more. Downsizing and reengineering have made many an organization seem a little brusque or discourteous. Their behavior lacks civility. If you ask people why their manners are so bad, they generally complain that they are overworked and overstressed.

But when it comes down to individual human beings—when it comes down to *you*—no one gets off the hook. The people you offend will vividly remember your bad manners. So take the time to thank an assistant for staying late or apologize to a colleague if you interrupt him at a meeting. Manners still count—a lot. When he was at Chrysler, finance executive Chris Steffen would always take the time to write a thank-you note to a helpful employee and then send a copy to the employee's superior. Steve Miller, a genius at putting together financial deals at Chrysler, made sure he would speak to your boss personally about how your work had benefited him. Dick Goeken, president of synthetic fuels at the former Gulf Oil, would not only see your boss but stop in and see you to express his appreciation directly. In today's organization, Steffen, Miller, and Goeken might be the exceptions. But they would probably get better results from their people than managers without manners.

If you have bad manners, you'll pay. Bill Agee, chief executive officer at the former Bendix and then at Morrison-Knudsen, created the perception that he had bad manners. Bill is actually a very gracious man, but at Bendix he promoted Mary Cunningham, a woman he later married, and many in the organization thought that was bad form. Then, at Morrison-Knudsen, rumors got around that Agee didn't like Boise, Idaho, where the organization was located, and his decision to run the organization from California seemed to confirm the rumors. The troops considered that bad manners, too. In both cases, Agee was damaged.

If you are among those handing out the unkind treatment, you will be hurt—and so will your organization. When employees deal harshly with one another, personality clashes become routine. That poisons the atmosphere and drains productivity. Today, bad manners is one of the biggest productivity killers in the work world. A subordinate who has been spoken to abruptly by a superior could obsess about it for days, bad-mouth the boss on the grapevine, and treat him with frosty reserve. All that drains time and energy from his work.

Some young people I know are taking extra time to be polite in the workplace. I see this strategy as paying off for them in a major way. People don't like to be treated poorly. They especially don't want to be treated poorly by someone younger than they are. Good manners burnish your reputation throughout the company and your profession.

QUESTIONS OF MANNERS

In writing her books, Miss Manners didn't go up on a mountain like Moses and bring down two tablets with the Ten Commandments of manners. Rather, she and other experts looked at their experiences, took into account the mores of the era, and described how they would handle something. For you, though, the approach they recommend might not always be right. Young people see the world in unique ways. You could probably produce a best-seller if you were to issue your own guide to manners for young people.

That book doesn't exist yet, so I've put together this section. It focuses on questions people in your generation have asked me about manners. I have tried to put myself in your shoes. If you disagree with my interpretations, I hope that you'll share your thinking with me.

Through the grapevine I've heard that my boss is getting fired. How should I act toward her?
Well, how would you like your subordinates to act toward you in this situation? You'd probably want to be treated with respect and sensitivity as long as you're the boss. You wouldn't appreciate people spreading the rumor that you're about to get canned. And when the ax did fall, you'd want subordinates to say they're sorry about the situation and offer to help. Also, you would want people to speak well of you after you leave.

I wonder about the proper etiquette for e-mail.
Many of the same principles that pertain to written communication and phone calls pertain to e-mail. That means, use appropriate language and proper grammar. Many young people seem to believe that the rules of grammar are suspended in e-mail. They are not, especially if your message is job-related. Similarly, avoid the use of emoticons (☺) and abbreviations (LOL). Reply as quickly as you can, but give the people you have e-mailed a break if they don't do the same. Many people, myself included, get hundreds of e-mails a day, and sometimes it just isn't possible to respond immediately. Don't forward e-mails thoughtlessly. Don't hit "reply all" unless you absolutely must. Most of all, remember that e-mail is not private. You never know when someone will decide to forward your immortal words to the entire world.

There I was at the fax machine, waiting for a fax from my client. Bored, I started to read another fax coming

through. The woman who was receiving the fax really chewed me out. What did I do wrong?
Think about it: Would you like your colleagues reading faxes that came to you? Of course not. Many faxes are semi-confidential. Act accordingly.

Can I send a memo to a client?
No. Memos are intended for internal distribution. When communicating with a client, you would send a formal letter. Some firms do send memos to clients, but it's considered bad form.

I went to the most boring speech at the Chamber of Commerce. Isn't it good manners for the speaker to try to make the talk interesting?
Yes. Before preparing the speech, speakers should ask themselves: "What can I say to this audience that will make this half hour spent with me useful to them?" It's common courtesy not to waste other people's time. On the other hand, it's also good manners to appear interested in what the speaker has to say.

I have had lunch with people who used their smartphones throughout the meal to make calls or send messages. Isn't that rude?
Yes. Such behavior is only permissible if the matter is truly urgent and the caller asks your permission to interrupt the lunch to make the call.

I had a job interview, and I didn't send a follow-up letter. I figured that I'd made all the points I wanted to make in the interview. But some people say I was wrong.
A follow-up letter is a good idea, because it gives the organization feedback on how you perceived the interview, and it also signals that you're interested in the job. Some type the letter; some send a handwritten note. Either way, it should go through the mail, not electronically—unless there is real urgency in the interviewing process, or they specifically ask you to get back to them immediately.

I don't know what to wear on "casual" Friday.
Proper attire on "casual" or "dress-down" day depends on the organizational culture. In some organizational cultures, blue jeans are okay. In others, people are more formal and wear slacks with a blazer. Look around the office and notice what the up-and-comers are wearing. That should be your guide.

I noticed that no one talked business at a company wine-and-cheese party. So I didn't either. Should I have said something about my work? My boss's boss was there.
Again, behavior depends on the organizational culture. At many organizations it's considered gauche to discuss professional matters at a social function. At others, such as start-up firms, *everything* involves business. Take your cue from your more experienced colleagues, and particularly from those who are above you in the office hierarchy. If everyone is talking about Hollywood blockbusters or holiday plans, I would hesitate before sharing your thoughts about inventory or quality control. But if everyone is enthusiastically analyzing an aspect of the business, feel free to chime in.

I have trouble with small talk. What's proper professional protocol?
Focus on topics that are of interest to everyone and keep the small talk light and positive. No one wants to hear complaints or critiques. It's also important that small talk doesn't offend. Slamming another religion, ethnicity, or gender will only make people uncomfortable, even if they are not members of that group. Better to talk about "safe" topics, such as sports or restaurants.

Before you go to an event, make sure you are up-to-date on current events. Another guest might ask what you thought of the president's speech or the Dow Jones Average or the latest political scandal. Being abreast of the news makes small talk easier.

How should I conduct myself at a meeting?

Again, the organizational culture will dictate most of your behavior. For instance, at some companies junior members aren't encouraged to talk at meetings. But no matter what the organizational culture, there is a basic etiquette for meetings.

Arrive on time, and don't leave early. If that's not possible, don't disrupt the group with your comings and goings. Treat everyone's input with respect. Don't monopolize the conversation. Make sure your comments are helpful. People know when you're talking just to talk, and that wastes their time.

When you go to a professional lunch or dinner, how much actual professional material should be discussed?

As much as the most powerful person at the table wants. That person will also have the authority to decide when the professional discussion should begin. Follow that person's lead.

I'm always on a diet, so I order salads at professional lunches. Unfortunately, they're tough to eat. What should I do?

Salads *are* tough to eat. And if you're struggling with the salad, it's bound to make your colleagues at the table uncomfortable. Fortunately, there are other low-calorie, low-fat entrées that are less of a challenge. You might try fish or a cottage cheese plate.

If you are on a diet, you can usually call ahead for the restaurant to have a special meal for you. This is becoming increasingly common. I usually let them know ahead of time that I want seafood without butter.

I sense you're damned in an office if you talk about your off-the-job social life, and damned if you don't. In the first instance, people have the dirt on you. In the latter case, people think you're secretive. What should I do?

It's an unavoidable fact of professional life that you are going to be judged. Anything you say about your interests or your lifestyle will be grist for the gossip mill. Therefore, be discreet.

The easiest way to judge what to disclose is to consider the office culture. In that culture would it be okay to discuss a marathon weekend of sex? Probably not. But what about a weekend spent watching a *Star Trek* marathon? Before you reveal anything, put it through the organizational-culture test. How would this information be viewed in this organization?

Also, remember that whatever you decide to disclose about yourself could have ramifications—good and bad—on your image. If you've spent the weekend fixing up houses in a low-income neighborhood, coworkers might perceive you as a good citizen . . . or as a bleeding-heart liberal. Remember that not everyone shares your values.

It's also good manners not to make anyone at work uncomfortable. If for any reason your lifestyle might upset others, keep it quiet.

Things to Remember

- Good manners give you a competitive edge
- Manners are really about the Golden Rule
- Your values determine your manners
- People respond strongly to good manners—and bad manners
- Spend some time researching manners

13

AFTER A SETBACK

This chapter is must reading IF:

- You've ever had a setback
- You blame yourself entirely for that setback
- You're angry
- You're just plain scared

If you've already had a career setback, thank your lucky stars. That puts you ahead of the game. Give me several job candidates side by side, and I'm likely to choose the one who's hit a few bumps in the road. That person tends to be more alert, tolerant, and pragmatic than a candidate who hasn't experienced a dark night of the soul. Early setbacks encourage you to sort out what success really means for you. Had you not had that setback, you might be blindly following conventional wisdom about career paths or assuming that your career strategies are invulnerable.

A setback also puts you in some excellent company. Winston Churchill, Lee Iacocca, and Steve Jobs all suffered major setbacks and then went on to amazing triumphs. In *Churchill: A Study in Failure,* Robert James emphasizes that from 1929 through September 1939, Churchill held no public office, and many people perceived him as an utter failure. He then went on to become one of Great Britain's greatest war leaders. Lee Iacocca was fired from Ford Motor Company and was thought to be no longer a player in the automotive world. Then, in the late 1970s, he came back to lead the Chrysler turnaround and became a legend in his own time. Steve Jobs was ousted from Apple. His next company never really got off the ground. But he returned to glory via his computer-animation firm, Pixar. And his second term at Apple was a triumph.

Setbacks frequently are a transformational force. They can turn the average person into a tiger.

OPPORTUNITY

George Daly, who is dean emeritus and professor of the McDonough School of Business at Georgetown University, deals with a lot of successful people. Most, if not all of them, he says, suffered setbacks—and used that bleak experience as an opportunity to move forward. "Successful people," he observes, "learn from their setbacks and become even more determined."

Today, because of the volatility of the global economy, we're seeing more and more setbacks. Back when I started my career, the business world was highly predictable. You went to work in a large organization, and, unless you were a roaring incompetent, you climbed the ladder to increasing levels of money, power, and prestige. On the other hand, the few who managed to get themselves fired became pariahs. Being fired had a terrific stigma attached to it in those days. Fortunately, that is no longer the case.

Getting canned has become almost a rite of passage in this brave new world of global business. In addition, you're more apt to have failures on your watch—just read business publications. That new product or service doesn't work out. The reorganization you helped orchestrate doesn't increase profits. Your management style irks some employees, they bail out, and the media starts talking about a brain drain at your company.

In short, if you're alive and working at this point in history,

you're bound to have a setback. What matters is not the setback, per se. It's how you work your way through it.

George Daly has some interesting insights on setbacks, especially since he worked through at least one himself. I have, too.

INTERVIEW: GEORGE DALY

RLD: In the circles where you travel, are you seeing more pro-
       fessional setbacks today?

GD: There's no question that there's more turbulence in busi-
       ness, and that tends to produce more setbacks. But I al-
       ways argue: For every setback, there's an *opportunity*.

RLD: Could you explain how setbacks can be opportunities?

GD: The key is to be able to learn from the setback. Not only
       can you learn from a setback—you *should* learn from it.

RLD: Do young people, because they're relatively new to the
       work world, tend to take a setback harder than a mature
       person?

GD: It depends. I think, on the average, yes. But there's a lot
       of variation. We can all remember when we were young
       and it seemed as if the world was ending when a girl
       broke up with us. However, I also know some fairly se-
       nior people who have had setbacks, and some of them
       have reacted very poorly. I believe that a setback is often
       a kind of defining moment for people. It literally is sort
       of a test of character, and we see what the person is
       made of.

RLD: In an ideal world, how should young people react to a
       setback? Perhaps they came in second for a job, were
       passed over for promotion, or were let go in a down-
       sizing.

GD: The first thing young people can do is let off steam: Get
       out there and talk about what happened. I think that the

biggest problems occur with setbacks when we bottle up the whole thing within ourselves and don't talk to others. When you talk about it with others, you get some perspective. For example, you realize you're not the first person in the world to have a setback.

RLD: In addition to venting, what else should young people do?

GD: They need to reflect on what the experience means. A good example of this is the person who loses a job and is shocked; this person claims not to have seen the signals. This is significant and needs to be looked at.

In my line of work I have terminated a fair number of people. If they're shocked—if they didn't see it coming—then I consult with their superiors. I ask, "Was this person alerted to the fact that their performance wasn't adequate?" I check over the personnel record. It has never happened that signals weren't sent. The person just didn't pick up on them. And that's why these people have to look at themselves. Why the tunnel vision? For this reason, we send those we dismiss to extensive outplacement counseling. During counseling they have the opportunity to examine how they see the world.

RLD: What about your personal experience with setbacks?

GD: I'm not atypical; I've had my share of setbacks. The one that comes to mind is the time when I was competing for a job. I *really* wanted that job. The search was narrowed down to a small group of finalists. Going into the last set of interviews, I might have been the favorite. And I felt that the last set of interviews had gone well. In fact, I went home thinking I had the job. Well, they chose someone else.

RLD: What did you do about that?

GD: I retraced my steps through the whole job interview process and took a look at how I had presented myself versus how I perceived I was presenting myself. I contacted some members of the job search committee to give me feedback. As a result of that analysis, I think that I'm a more effective professional—and person.

RLD: Thanks for sharing that. My setback was a little different. I had been with a large organization for twenty-plus years. Then there were changes. I was forced to look at myself and ask if the corporate world was still for me. That took a lot of soul-searching. I was terrified of reconfiguring my career path. I was also angry that outside forces were pushing me toward change. So I did what Dwight Eisenhower used to do. When he was angry with someone, he wrote down that person's name and put it in a drawer. He let some time pass and then pulled out the piece of paper. Over time, the name lost its hold on him.

I ultimately decided not to seek another job in another large corporation. What I really wanted was to try my hand at running my own business. Had I not had a setback, I would never have experienced the absolute high of being an entrepreneur. I would still have been in that old, comfy, corporate cocoon and probably not growing. A setback delivers a message that you *have* to pay attention to.

I was wondering, though: Can future setbacks be prevented?

GD: Absolutely not. Setbacks have always been with us and always will be with us. With the volatility of the global marketplace, there will just be more of them. But that also means there will be more opportunities.

THE FAILURE TABOO

For many years America was not a good place in which to have a setback. As John Ward points out in *Song of the Phoenix: The Hidden Rewards of Failure,* our Calvinistic roots made us phobic about failure. That was for two reasons. One, the tenets of Calvinism held that God rewarded good people with material success. Therefore, if you weren't succeeding, you probably weren't a good person. The holiest person in church was the person with the most material goods. Two, according to Calvinism, your profession was considered sacred. If you were an accountant or a nurse, that was as sacred a vocation as being a member of the clergy. This meant that everything that affected your profession was viewed in a serious light.

Screwing up professionally thus had dire implications. Therefore, when people did screw up, they tended to try to keep it quiet. Talk about failure might be among the last taboos left in America. But when Lee Iacocca was introduced at a college lecture as "having left Ford and gone to Chrysler," Iacocca, the iconoclast, took on the failure taboo. He strode right to the podium and said, "I didn't leave Ford. I was fired." And he brought the house down.

In the media there are lots of stories of comebacks—but not too many articles about people when they're struggling to come back. In *Complete and Utter Failure,* Neil Steinberg observes that "those who fail, who come in second, whose sales figures disappoint" are quickly eliminated from our radar screens. We have tended not to deal with them anymore.

But all that has been changing. It had to. There are now just too many of us who fail, come in second, or disappoint. I prepare the staff in our agency—as I do my two sons—for failure as well as for success. And when I think about my successful colleagues and what they were doing over the past five years, there isn't one of them who hasn't had some kind of defeat.

I believe it was in the late 1980s, about the time downsizing became the new modus operandi of business, that the stigma associated with failure began to lose some of its power. Churches in posh suburbs like Westport, Connecticut, began to offer support groups for unemployed executives. Some of those executives allowed themselves to be interviewed by the media: They actually *talked* about being out of work. In 1987, Carole Hyatt and Linda Gottlieb's book *When Smart People Fail* openly discussed failure and named names of those who had failed. The book's stance was not that, if you failed, you were a bad person; instead, the authors contended that failure was the result of being in the wrong niche. The typical failure was the entrepreneurial type who was stuck in a buttoned-down organization—and not doing well. I knew hundreds of people who fit that description.

Today, failure is not just out of the closet; it's coming to be perceived as a character builder. That's why a failure early in your career can ultimately be beneficial. Failure can motivate you to alter your direction or to get back on track. It can be energizing. It can make you savvier about the world and smarter about your own habits, weaknesses, and approach. Are there ways in which you may have contributed to your own demise? Probably—but you don't have to make those mistakes again.

Clearly, failure has become more acceptable. The question is: Are you willing to accept and learn from your failures?

MAKING SETBACKS WORK FOR YOU

How can you tap into the power of a setback—and make it work for you? I have nine recommendations.

1. *If you're shocked by the setback, ask yourself why.* In *Ambition: How We Manage Success and Failure Throughout Our Lives,* Gilbert Brim observes that "sometimes we don't know we are losing until the very end." And that's not entirely our fault. In a nation of optimists, there's reluctance to deliver bad news. It's the courageous supervisor—and the equally courageous colleague—who will even hint that there are major problems. Oh, sure, there are signals: Your work comes back from the new powers-that-be with plenty of red pencil, and something in your gut says the new regime and you aren't on the same wavelength. But it's not unusual for the brass not to spell out that there's a problem. When it comes to bad news, your colleagues are usually equally evasive. Then one day, seemingly out of the blue, someone in command says, "This just isn't working out."

You can avoid the shock, and perhaps even prevent the setback from happening, if you develop the ability and the willingness to read the subtext beneath the surface. It's best to consider *everything* in the workplace as symbolic. If you're not invited to a meeting, ask yourself what that means. If you don't receive a raise, ask what that could represent. If the bosses are consistently impatient with you and act as if you really get under their skin, ask yourself or a trusted colleague what might be going on.

If this looming setback can't be prevented, don't waste time in denial. Your first few phone calls should be to those who've gone through similar ordeals. Those kinds of conversations bring home to you that you're not unique and that, yes, people do survive your particular kind of setback. Even before the setback occurs, start thinking about how to deal with it from a position of strength. Certainly you might want to consult a lawyer. But think seriously about all your options.

2. *Be gentle with yourself.* Setbacks can happen to anyone. Winston Churchill lost elections. So did Abraham Lincoln. Walt Disney's first animation studio went bankrupt. Billionaire Michael Bloomberg, three-time mayor of New York City, was fired from Salomon Brothers. Anna Wintour, before becoming editor of *Vogue,* was fired from *Harper's Bazaar.* And do you remember Facebook's disastrous IPO? Anyone can take a dive. So give yourself a break.

3. *Don't play the blame game.* Were you treated unfairly? Perhaps so. It happens. Unfortunately, no matter how angry you may be, you gain nothing by blaming others. Failure can be a springboard to success, but only if you are willing to put blame aside and consider whether you may have inadvertently contributed to the setback. That's the only way you can hope to avoid similar crashes in the future. But even there, it's self-destructive and inaccurate to blame yourself entirely, for forces may be at work that have nothing to do with you. The best approach might be to take the advice of the great Roman emperor Marcus Aurelius. He said (in *The Emperor's Handbook*), "If you fail, blame only yourself, or better yet, don't blame anyone." It was true in the second century, and it's true now. Analyze; don't blame.

4. *Get feedback.* Everyone feels vulnerable after a setback, so it isn't easy to ask for feedback, even from friends and allies. But this could be the single most enlightening step you take. At the very least, doing this will let you know what people might be saying about you. And because you're in a crisis, you'll find that people will tend to be straight with you.

After she was selected for the first wave of layoffs at a major food company, a member of the Public Relations department did a smart thing. She went to one of her colleagues and asked why she had been let go. She knew there was a message there but just didn't know exactly what it was. The colleague was candid and told her she was a poor fit for corporate life. "But I have never had trouble with senior management," she said. "And aren't they the ones who count?"

The colleague then gave her an education on how images are formed in an organization, pointing out that the reason she had gotten by with senior executives was probably because their interaction with her was so limited. "You couldn't sustain being a good corporate citizen" was the way the colleague summed up her situation. Believe it or not, this was the first inkling she had that perhaps she didn't belong in this type of organization. And, by ultimately leading her to a more hospitable work setting, this setback changed her life.

5. *Be open to alternatives,* even if they're not directly related to your current career path. A media representative who was laid off decided to try out her long-term dream of selling for a living. She realized that a lot of the skills she used in pitching stories to the media could be used in sales. She turned out to be more successful in sales than she had been in media relations.

Many layoffs occur because you are in a declining industry or a shrinking profession. Once you're out of it, the playing field seems more level, and you begin to do well.

6. *Keep it simple.* Much of the advice you get during this crisis might seem simplistic. And it is. On the other hand, your problem might seem very complex to you. But it probably isn't. One man was put on probation at his job and assumed it was because he had deep-seated issues with authority. A colleague let him in on a little secret: "You can't stand the boss, and it shows." The solution to the problem was not for the man to figure out why he hated the boss; it was simply for the man not to be so open in showing his feelings. If you think the interpretations people give you for why you suffered a setback are simplistic, keep listening; they're probably just cutting through all the psychobabble and giving you the truth.

7. *Move toward the future.* The last place where you want to be stuck is in your current problem. That's why so many people get active after a setback. They want to see movement. They want change. They go on diets, learn new computer skills, travel to San Francisco to see if they would like to relocate there, develop a whole new network, start new exercise regimes. Activities like these allow their frame of reference to shift to *post*-setback.

8. *Realize you're not the first person to be scared.* You have plenty of company. Also, realize that fear is usually a friend; it warns us to be careful. Fear becomes the enemy only when we allow it to control us. If you're becoming overly scared, call up someone who has been in your shoes and is now doing just fine.

9. *Refrain from becoming preoccupied with setbacks.* Sure, you'll learn a lot about failure when you're past it. But your goal is to go through it and not be fixated on failure. It's just one part of your professional experience—with luck, a small part.

Things to Remember

- Setbacks can be opportunities
- Don't isolate after a setback
- Don't take full blame for the setback
- Don't become preoccupied with a setback

14

MENTORS

This chapter is a must read IF:

- You're wondering what a mentor is and whether you need one
- You're outgrowing your current mentor
- You suspect there's a downside to the whole "mentor" thing
- You don't know how to get a mentor
- You feel alone
- You realize you need help

Mentorship has been getting a lot of press in the past few years. It has inspired books, articles, websites, and a long list of corporate programs. There's even a National Mentoring Month (January). People have figured out that having a mentor can make all the difference.

Warren Buffett had one. Jay-Z had one. So did Larry Page and Sergey Brin of Google, Sheryl Sandburg of Facebook, Tom Hanks, Oprah Winfrey, designer Vera Wang, and Mahatma Gandhi. In fact, virtually every successful person has had some kind of mentor. The mentor could have been Mom or Dad, the football coach, a math professor, or the chief executive officer of the company. In *The Mentor Connection,* Michael G. Zey cites a

Heidrick & Struggles study of 1,250 senior executives whose names had appeared in the "Who's News" section of the *Wall Street Journal*. Two-thirds of them said that they had had a mentor—and of that two-thirds, a third had had *two or more* mentors. And, not surprisingly, a number of you have told me that you need mentors.

In this chapter, I'll discuss what mentoring is. I'll interview my former mentor, Walter Seifert, who taught communications for twenty-four years at Ohio State University and helped thousands of kids get jobs. I'll discuss the benefits and pitfalls of the mentoring process. And I'll give recommendations on how you can attract the right mentor for you.

WHAT IS A MENTOR?

Most mentors and protégés have their own ideas as to what mentoring is about. A mentor might be a teacher, a parent, or someone you admire who acts as a role model. A mentor can be someone who encourages you in a general way or someone in your office who knows the specific issues and can guide you through the political minefield. A mentor could be someone you meet with formally or informally. It could be someone who acts as an advisor for many years or someone who helps you navigate through a single project. Michael Zey defines a mentor as someone who oversees someone else's career and development through "teaching, counseling, providing psychological support, protecting, and at times promoting or sponsoring" that person.

At the beginning of the relationship, it's useful for you and the mentor to articulate what the parameters of the relationship will be. For example, you might be assuming that you'll get help with day-to-day office politics, when the mentor intends to restrict the relationship to meeting for lunch once a month and encouraging you. Also, the parameters might change during the relationship. Your mentor may become too busy to offer broad-based support anymore or, conversely, may acquire a position of power and be able to help you more than ever. This relationship is fluid.

On the other hand, there are many mentoring relationships in which nothing is made explicit. The relationship just sort of happens, and neither you nor your mentors comment on the nature of the relationship.

MULTIPLE MENTORS

To get what you need, you might require more than one mentor. The mentor relationship isn't like marriage. It's not necessarily supposed to last for life. And it isn't monogamous; you can have two or more mentors at the same time. For a long time my mentor was my dad. Then I graduated from college and wasn't sure what I wanted to do. I found my number two mentor when I went to Ohio State for graduate school in communications. In addition to being an inspiring professor, Walter Seifert was active in the profession. He started the Public Relations Student Society of America (PRSSA) in 1967. Then he went on to found the educators' section of the PRSSA and later was chosen as outstanding teacher by the organization. Although he has died since I interviewed him for the first edition of this book, his words hold up. Trust me: You can't go wrong taking his advice.

INTERVIEW: WALTER SEIFERT

RLD: How would you define this entity we call "mentoring"?
WS: I think of mentoring in simple terms. It's helping another person succeed.
RLD: Do you think mentoring is necessary to success?
WS: As I look back over my own career and the careers of my best students, it certainly appears that they—and I—got more help from the outside than from within ourselves.

For example, one of my big breaks came through a mentor.

I was working as the night editor for a newspaper syndicate in Cleveland called Central Press. During the day I would fish in Lake Erie. One day I caught half a bushel of fish. I cleaned them and brought them into the syndicate. Everybody got some. Well, the editor came out of his office and said, "Mr. Seifert, I think you ought to write a fishing column." Thanks to him, I wrote a fishing column that appeared in a hundred newspapers. It was called "Fish Tales." And "Fish Tales" got me a trip to Bermuda. I met my wife in Bermuda and got a job there as a director of public relations—all because someone took the time to guide me.

RLD: How did you get to Ohio State?

WS: The head of the journalism school wanted to introduce some public relations courses. Over twenty-four years, I've had 10,000 students. I think they wanted me because I had actually worked in the profession. And that's what a good mentor has to do—know the field from hands-on experience. Too many educators know their areas of expertise from books rather than experience.

RLD: What are the benefits of having a mentor?

WS: A mentor can tell you about a field, because the mentor has had a deep relationship with that field. Also, the mentor can assess your potential in that field. The mentor can make a judgment about whether you have the horsepower for the field. In addition, if the mentor is like me, the mentor can help young people get jobs in the field. I've been able to help a number of young people get jobs, but I'd place them only if they were strong in their field.

RLD: So you consider finding jobs for people part of your mentoring activities?

WS: Yes, at least their first job. That's the toughest to get. But I also consider it part of my role to discourage weak candidates from entering the field. I felt that that was also my responsibility.

RLD: Has there been any negative fallout from your mentoring?

WS: Probably the biggest fallout was the disapproval of some of my teaching colleagues. Some saw my mentoring work with students as a waste of time.

RLD: I've heard horror stories about mentor relationships that go on too long. For instance, the protégé outgrows the mentor or becomes more successful than the mentor. Do some mentors hold on too long?

WS: Certainly. As far as I know, I haven't had that problem. I enjoy following someone's career, and often that's gone on for years. In fact, for fifteen years I had a newsletter called *Jewel Club Newsletter*. It was for all those I had mentored. In it I brought people up to date on everyone's accomplishments. Once a year, I ran a contest. Readers were to submit their best work, and the winners would get a prize.

If someone doesn't want to keep in touch with a mentor, though, that's something you can spot right away, and you leave that person alone. And there are points in someone's development when that person needs a different type of mentor. I use the analogy of medicine. Usually you start out with a general practitioner, but often you need a specialist. So you go from the generalist to the specialist, and you get what you need. As you rise in your profession, you'll get more sophisticated mentors who are on top of the field you're now in or will be in.

RLD: How would you advise a young person to find a mentor?

WS: A bright young person should survey the environment and find out who can be of help. It's best to find local people. If, for example, you want to enter public relations, then you should survey those you know in public relations. When you've selected someone you want to approach, ask this person if he or she could answer a few questions for you. That could lead to a relationship, even a job. If there are no public relations people you can talk to in your environment, then go to the library, look up the names of public relations people, and contact them with questions. See where that leads.

RLD: What do you get out of the mentoring relationship?

WS: Personally, I enjoy watching young people develop. Every time one of "my kids" has a success, I feel a tremendous degree of satisfaction. For example, Bob, when you publish a book, I feel very happy for you.

RLD: Thanks, Walt. It was you who helped me get a sense of who I was and who I could be professionally. You also guided me to see what my strengths were. I couldn't believe you thought I had so many!

WHAT'S IN IT FOR YOU?

For me, Walter Seifert was the Mr. Chips of the mentoring world. But the benefits you get from mentoring might not include a Mr. Chips–type relationship. It might be much more businesslike, especially if your organization assigns you a mentor. A number of organizations now provide high-potential people with mentors. Your mentor may tell it exactly like it is and not be sensitive to your feelings. Some of my best mentors didn't sugarcoat their criticism of me. What was valuable to me was the input they gave, not the relationship, per se.

I remember another one of my early professional mentors, the late Ed Doherty. Ed was a great person and a splendid writer. Once he gave me an assignment, and I turned in what I thought was a first-rate job. Doherty called me into his office. "What nationality are you?" he asked.

"American," I said.

"Oh, I'm sure you have deep roots in another culture," he said.

Proud of my German-Irish heritage, I told him he was right.

Doherty smiled and said, "Well, that explains why you can't yet write English." I was mortified. Doherty then sat me down and took me through what I had written word by word. Later he bought me *Fowler's Modern English Usage, The Elements of Style* by E. B. White, and *Roget's Thesaurus.* I will never forget Ed Doherty—and what he did for me in those moments when I was full of myself.

A mentor's oldest role has probably been socialization of the protégé. As young people entered the workforce or started their own business, they needed to learn how to act in those particular environments. Mentors would tell them not to wear a plaid jacket to work, not to talk about business at a company social function, and to be deferential to everyone. If the protégé was an entrepreneur, the socialization process might include education about matters that are pertinent to the entrepreneurial culture, such as keeping a low profile with clients, not complaining, and not letting nonentrepreneurs know that self-employment isn't always wonderful.

Another benefit of having a mentor is having a role model. Former President Bill Clinton found one in his high school bandleader—and also in his mother. I found one in my dad and later in Walter Seifert. Some find it in a professor, in their first boss, or in an assigned mentor. (That's how President Barack Obama met Michelle: He was an intern at a law firm, and she was a first-year associate assigned to be his mentor.) You might even choose as your "virtual mentor" someone you will probably never meet, such as a celebrity, an accomplished professional at the top of your field, or a figure from history, such as Marcus Aurelius or Winston Churchill. That may sound foolish, but it's amazing how clarifying it can be to ask yourself, what would that person do in this situation?

A third benefit of having a mentor can be receiving candid advice about what to do in order to succeed—and what not to do. Your mentor may tell you, for example, not to kill yourself writing reports for your boss, because your boss has little actual power, and no one else is going to see the reports; instead, he or she might advise you to spend more of your time learning about finance and acquiring new skills.

A fourth benefit is the protection you may receive. As you try to increase your power and influence, mentors can use *their* power and influence to keep your enemies and competitors from attacking you. This is a biggie. Without protection, many successful people wouldn't have been able to expand their turf in their business.

A fifth benefit is promotion, or sponsoring. Mentors can pave the way for your advancement. If there's a vice presidency open, they can lobby to help you get it. In a sense, mentors can be your public relations agents. They can talk you up to all the right people. And if they have sufficient power, they can actually pull strings so that you can advance. Mentors have even been known to create jobs for their protégés.

Other benefits that mentors may sometimes provide are emotional support, a sense of belonging, and a chance to vent. But don't count on that. With the work environment now so chaotic, some of the "softer" parts of mentoring have been tossed overboard, and many such relationships have become much more straightforward.

WHAT'S IN IT FOR THE MENTOR?

What are the benefits to mentors? Why do they bother doing it? Well, there is the satisfaction Walter Seifert discussed. Mentoring usually gives the mentor a sense of accomplishment.

Also, there is an expectation in many fields that professionals, as they mature or become successful, will pass on what they know to others. Those others don't necessarily have to be younger than they; an overnight success who's only twenty-four would still be expected to share know-how with people who might be in their fifties. People who don't participate in this ritual of passing on their expertise are open to censure that they're "all get and no give."

In addition, there is usually prestige associated with mentoring. If your protégé makes it big-time, your status may be enhanced as well.

Another benefit is the reciprocal help that protégés can sometimes offer mentors. Part of that help is in terms of information; the protégé can be the eyes and ears of the mentor. Another form of help could be sharing resources. For instance, mentors might not have the technical expertise the protégé has.

Another benefit for mentors is that your protégés can increase your sphere of influence. Having a protégé in marketing and another in finance can extend your tentacles throughout the organization.

THE DOWNSIDE

There are a number of potential drawbacks in the mentor–protégé relationship, too. They include:

A mismatch. Problems can arise when your mentor's values differ from your own, when you don't admire the way your mentor does business, when your mentor seems unavailable, or, alternatively, when he or she hovers too closely. Maybe you don't like your mentor (or—worse—you suspect that your mentor doesn't like you). Or maybe the two of you just lack chemistry. That can happen.

It's also possible that you have chosen someone who initially strikes you as an ideal role model but turns out to be anything but. Or a mentor who is perfect for you in the early days of your career may have less to offer a few years down the road. Sometimes you have to move on. And sometimes you need more than one mentor. Nothing wrong with that.

Lost confidence. An article in *Inc.* magazine described how veteran entrepreneur Ric Leichtung sent several pages of single-spaced criticism to junior entrepreneur Steve Leveen analyzing Leveen's promotional material.

Leveen felt the critique was right on the money, and Leichtung became his mentor.

But the story might not have had such a happy ending. I know a woman who went from a nonprofit to the private sector. A well-meaning executive at the corporation tried to help her adjust. Unfortunately, the barrage of advice from the would-be mentor undermined the woman's confidence in her own ability to decode the environment. It's fifteen years later, and I don't think this woman has recovered yet. Too much input was delivered too quickly—and with no "sandwich," i.e., no praise surrounding and softening the criticism.

Overdependency. You never want to depend on your mentor too much. Mentors are supposed to be a bridge to what you hope to achieve, not a Big Daddy or an Earth Mother. I vividly remember a woman in graduate school who came from an inferior college. She was lost at Ohio State and not doing well. Then her thesis advisor "adopted" her. She blossomed, and her grades got much better. But she couldn't—or didn't want to—break the hold the professor had on her. She evolved into a mini-version of him.

The worst thing about becoming too dependent on a mentor is that you stunt your own growth. I advise young people who are in such a relationship to get out— but get out nicely. You don't want an enemy on your hands.

Guilt by association. Your mentor may lose power, retire, or screw up. And that could reflect on you. Smart protégés avoid this situation by not becoming too closely identified with a single mentor. Instead, they maintain a number of mentors in the organization. Political alliances always involve political risk.

Speeding ahead of the mentor. It happens. Your mentor is a director, and then you're appointed senior director or vice president. There could be hard feelings.

This is best handled ahead of time, while the promotion
is still in the works. Discuss with your mentors the
benefits that could come to them from your promotion.
Outgrowing your mentors is a common occurrence.
Your focus has to be on not injuring the mentor's
feelings.

Betrayal. It's not unusual for mentors—or protégés—to
feel betrayed. Maybe you think they're not promoting
you enough. Maybe they judge that you're being too
independent. This is a tough situation. Perception is
perception. Often the relationship isn't salvageable. The
best you can do in such a case is defuse some of the
negative feelings and continue to treat the mentor with
respect.

Despite the possible pitfalls, I'm convinced that it's
better to have a mentor than to not have one. The best
advice I could give you is to be alert for changes in the
relationship. But how do you get a relationship going?
There are a number of ways.

GETTING A MENTOR

Before you approach anyone about being your mentor, focus
on the qualities you're seeking. Do you want someone who
knows the inside scoop? If so, you might choose a mentor who
is inside the company. One way to find such a person is to go to
the HR department, which may have an established mentorship program. (Among Fortune 500 companies, according to
the *Wall Street Journal,* fully 70 percent provide such programs.)
If you prefer someone outside of your office, go to a professional organization, attend a conference, or do an "Advanced
People Search" on LinkedIn. Once you have identified a potential mentor, prepare your pitch. This is your chance to present your accomplishments and to convince your would-be
mentor that you are on the way up. But be careful: Rather than
asking someone directly to be your mentor, a responsibility that

may sound onerous, keep it simple. Request specific advice on a particular project or issue. If they agree to discuss the matter with you, don't forget to send a thank-you note or e-mail. And be sure to get back to him or her with the results. Did you follow the advice you received? How did it go? Remember—you want to establish a relationship, so make sure the other person feels appreciated.

WHAT MENTORS WANT IN A PROTÉGÉ

In *The Mentor Connection,* Michael G. Zey looks at this issue from the mentor's point of view. Zey interviewed a number of executives and asked what they looked for in a protégé. What makes a protégé appropriate and valuable to a mentor? Zey lists ten qualities:

1. Intelligence
2. Ambition
3. Willingness—and ability—to deal with power and risk
4. Ability to ultimately perform the mentor's job
5. Loyalty
6. Sharing the mentor's perceptions about the organization and work
7. Dedication to the company
8. Political smarts
9. Positive perception of the company
10. Ability to form alliances

From these ten qualities, we can construct the profile of the ideal protégé.

• You are bright, eager to learn, and alert enough to pick up on what's happening in the global economy, the industry, the organization, and the department—but not so full of yourself that you feel you have all the answers
• Because you have a strong desire to get ahead, you are

able to understand the mentor's ambition and are willing
to make sacrifices to advance it
- You exhibit enough leadership to reassure the mentor that
  you can make and implement timely decisions
- You have the potential to jump in and take over the
  mentor's job responsibilities if necessary
- You can tell the good guys from the bad guys
- You share the same value system as the mentor
- You believe in the company
- You know how to get things done in an organization
- You understand how to put deals together

Things to Remember

- There's no fixed definition of what a mentor is "supposed"
  to be
- The protégé-mentor relationship is mutually useful
- Beware the pitfalls of being a protégé
- Mentors have certain qualities in mind when they select
  protégés

15

MOVING ON

This chapter is must reading IF:

- You want to change jobs but aren't sure it's a good move
- Your organization has family-friendly policies, but you still get accusing looks when you leave at 5:00 PM
- You don't feel you're learning on the job
- You're bored

The Organization Man, famous for his fidelity to the firm, looked for a good job and stayed for life. That rarely happens anymore. Today, according to the Bureau of Labor Statistics, people change jobs an average of eleven times between ages eighteen and forty-six. The message is clear: Many times throughout your working life you'll go through the gut-wrenching experience of leaving your job. In this chapter, my aim is to help ease that transition.

MY JOB-CHANGE STORY

A number of years ago I received an attractive job offer from Bob Malott, the chairman of FMC in Chicago—and one of *Fortune*'s "Toughest Bosses in America." At the time I was doing

very well at a large public relations agency in New York. I was
constantly hopping on planes to help clients all over the globe,
and I felt like a big cheese. Well, Malott made me feel even bigger. He was a wonderful guy, and I got the impression that he
thought I could walk on water. I accepted his offer, without
much thought. I was to report to work September 1.

Slowly it dawned on me that I had made a big mistake. At
FMC I would have only one client—FMC—whereas in the
agency business I had multiple clients and lots of action. And I
realized I wasn't ready to trade New York for Chicago. My
angst became so bad that I got up the nerve to call Bob Malott
and ask to be let off the hook. Fortunately, Bob was a gentleman about it. He even wished me good luck.

Lesson learned: Voluntarily changing jobs *should* be a tough
decision. If it isn't, you're not asking yourself the right questions. I never did something that dumb again.

A very able young man named Dwight worked for me.
Dwight had a great history of success in everything he did. But
it was clear that, no matter how hard he tried or how much he
did, he could never really shine in the public relations business.
He didn't have a feel for marketing. I called him in and told him
that he could stay with us, but it would be better for him if he
moved on. And I told him why. He protested. He told me he
wanted the job and could do well. Frankly, he was scared. Well,
Dwight spent two more years with us, but it was wasted time.
He shouldn't have done it. He did fine for us, but he didn't do
fine for himself. Lesson: Don't be scared to move on if, in your
heart, you know it's right.

Making that decision is not easy. For one thing, there are
usually valid reasons for staying. On the positive side, there may
be aspects of the job—the pay, the benefits, the location, the
prestige, the camaraderie—that you enjoy and that you think
will be difficult to replicate. On the negative side, the thought
of looking for a new job may fill you with dread. Who wants
to send out all those résumés, endure nerve-racking interviews,

and risk the very real possibility of being rejected? That prospect keeps many people stuck in jobs they can barely tolerate.

Deciding to leave one job and look for another takes courage and fortitude. But, if things are going badly at your current job, and you have the sense that that isn't going to change, starting anew is the right thing to do. How can you tell if the time has come to look around? Here are a few warning signs worth paying attention to.

WARNING SIGNS

Trust your instincts. If you suspect that things are not going well at work, you're probably right. Some clues are blatant, such as having a subordinate promoted above you or having your office—or your parking spot—taken away. When that happens, you know you're in trouble. Other indications are harder to assess, because they may seem accidental, such as being excluded from meetings or denied essential information. But the clearest indication of all that you should look for another job is the situation identified by headhunter Jean Allen, a partner in the search firm Heidrick & Struggles. I asked her, "How do you know when it's time to leave a job?"

And she answered, "You're miserable."

That is really all you need to know. If you are miserable, it doesn't matter how perfect the job might sound on paper. It doesn't matter if you are the envy of everyone you know or if your colleagues feel as if they won the lottery every time they clock in. If you don't feel the same, if you dread Mondays and can barely stand to breathe the same air as your boss, it's time to move on.

Other signs include the following:

You're not learning. This might sound minor—after all, you're not in school—but it's actually a huge issue. If you're not learning, you're not growing. And if you're not growing, the job is becoming routine, and boredom

is sure to set in. A fulfilling job, a job you can stay in,
offers challenges. It requires you to master new skills, to
try new techniques, to absorb new information, to meet
new people. If none of that is happening, you're
stagnating.

You can't seem to get an even break. When you
make an error, no matter how inconsequential it may be,
your boss jumps all over it. Meanwhile, your
contributions go unacknowledged. You haven't received
a raise or a promotion in a while, although others at your
level have, and the perks that other employees enjoy
somehow never come your way. Although you try to rise
above it, you can't shake the feeling that you are
unappreciated.

Your work isn't valued. The projects you are asked to
do are clearly not on anyone's list of priorities. You feel
inundated with busywork, yet you can't seem to get
assigned to anything else. Or perhaps you don't have
enough to do, and you worry that you're being sidelined.
You'd like to contribute more, if only they'd let you.
Your efforts seem futile. Your confidence is being eroded.

You're suffering emotionally or physically. Maybe
you're angry and frustrated and taking it out on your
friends and family because you can't express those feelings
at work. Maybe you're developing physical symptoms
that your doctor ascribes to stress or anxiety. Or maybe
you have what feels like a bad case of the blues. If you
suspect that your anger or hopelessness stems from your
job, it could be time to move on. (It might also be smart
to find a therapist to help you sort through it all.)

**Your values are not in sync with those of the
company.** Maybe the company plans to expand into
foreign markets, but you believe that profits should be
plowed back into the community. Or the company wants
to invest in oil and gas, but you, as an advocate of
greener forms of energy, such as solar and wind power,

object. It doesn't matter what the specific issues are. The point is this: If you often find yourself thinking, "That's not right," the fit between you and your job is no longer beneficial for either you or the company.

The business is in bad shape. Professionally, you're doing great, but you can see that your industry is in trouble. Now you're hearing ominous rumors about your company. There have already been layoffs—and to your relief you've made it through. But a steady stream of cost-cutting measures is alerting you to the company's continued downward trajectory. You are certain that sooner or later the ax will fall.

No job is perfect in every respect, and there are always going to be occasional rough periods. So you could probably learn to live with one or two of these factors. But if the problems are piling up, or you have the feeling that things are getting worse, it may be time to take the next step in your career.

WHAT NOT TO DO

NUMBER ONE: DO NOT QUIT YOUR JOB

Once you have determined that you want out, you may be tempted to bail immediately. Do not give in to this temptation. As counterintuitive as it may seem, employers prefer to hire people who already have jobs. Having a job means that someone else has checked you out and found you to be employable. You have essentially been vetted—whereas being unemployed, even if you quit your job of your own volition, raises the suspicion that you might be the kind of person who simply cannot hold down a job. That's an image you don't need. If possible, stay in your job while you're looking for another one.

NUMBER TWO: DON'T TELL ANYONE THAT YOU'RE ON THE MARKET UNTIL YOU MUST

Your campaign should be strictly stealth. Don't say anything at work. Don't make an announcement on Facebook. And don't conduct your job search via a company computer. That's a risk not worth taking. You're better off using your personal computer at home or going to the public library.

If, despite all your precautions, your boss does find out that you're on the market, stay calm and take the advice of John Johnstone, former chairman and CEO of Olin Corporation. "Basically, your response has to be, 'I'm trying to look outside to determine what's available.' Then you describe how you're not learning or contributing enough, whatever the situation is. That gives you a chance to talk about your role in the organization."

Occasionally, such a talk can be surprisingly productive. But that doesn't mean your problems are over. Jean Allen explains: "It can sometimes happen that you tell your company you're leaving, and they convince you to stay. But 80 percent of the time you will be out of there within a year, anyway. What happens is that the company just doesn't trust you as much anymore. The covenant has changed, and now they see you as a gun for hire. At the same time you have a different feeling about your value, and you may get a little cocky. Whatever happens, you're out of there in a year, anyway. So be careful! If you say you're going to leave, be sure you want to leave."

NEXT STEPS

FIGURE OUT YOUR OPTIONS

Do your research; vague impressions aren't enough. If you don't usually read the business section of the newspaper or industry journals, start doing so now. Know what's going on in the economy as a whole and in your industry in particular.

Look at job boards. Check out the competition. And be willing to consider a broader range of positions than you have in the past.

Update your résumé. Years may have passed since the last time you looked for a job, and you have undoubtedly acquired new skills. Make sure your résumé reflects that reality.

Activate your network. You should always be in touch with mentors and other people in your network, but if you've let that slide, now is the time to reconnect. However, don't appear desperate; it's not an effective strategy. It's better to be upbeat and positive every step of the way, including during interviews. Tempting though it may be to trash your current (or former) employer, it will only count against you. You must stay positive.

Assess your job skills—and your temperament. Begin by examining your current job in an objective way. Why has it been so stressful? Your first instinct might be to say that there is a personality conflict; you and your boss just don't hit it off. But is that actually the case? Maybe the problem is that you're in the wrong field, the wrong job, or the wrong sort of company. For instance, some people thrive in large multinational corporations such as GM or Microsoft or Coca-Cola. Others are more comfortable in smaller, more loosely structured businesses. Before you dump all the blame on your supervisor, consider the possibility that you would be happier in another kind of organization.

Apply for jobs—lots of jobs. But don't be in too much of a rush. You don't have to take the first job that comes along if you know it isn't right. Taking a job you think you are going to hate can be a huge mistake. Don't do it.

LEAVE ON GOOD TERMS

When you finally do get a job, leave the old one gracefully, no matter how stormy your tenure there may have been. If possible, you might even want to mend a few fences. Under no circumstances should you depart in a vengeful or nasty way. As Jean Allen says, "Life is long. Just remember that what feels really good when you're walking out the door will very possibly come back and bite you if you need a reference. The universe can catch up with you in many ways. Leave with class."

There are plenty of excellent reasons for leaving a job. There are also plenty of foolish reasons. One of the most invalid reasons I've encountered is the desire for a "perfect" job. Unfortunately, the "perfect job" is a self-destructive fantasy that leads to discontent and unnecessary job-hopping. And job-hopping can burn you out faster than a grueling job will. Trust me: There is no such thing as the perfect job.

William J. Kirby, senior vice president of FMC (the company I almost made a bad job-hopping move to), warns young people not to fall into the trap of believing that a new boss, more money, or a different type of organization will create that perfect job for you. The grass is rarely greener on the other side—it's just different. The closest you'll come to the perfect job is one that's a good fit for you. Focus on the fit, not on some imaginary criteria for what a perfect job *should* be.

Among the personal issues that should determine that fit are the organization's family-friendly policies. An organization that proclaims it has family-friendly policies and then gives dirty looks to mothers and fathers who depart at 5:00 PM is an organization to consider leaving.

I once interviewed for a job with a major fashion organization. The pay package was great. I would have reported directly to the CEO and had a large budget and millions of dollars of foundation money to give away. But a few days before I had to make my decision, one of the people in the organization bragged to me that he had electronically bugged his coworkers' offices and found out every little tidbit about them. I politely said no to the organization and have never mentioned that story until this book. For me, such an invasion of privacy—and an organizational culture that seemed to tolerate it—was reason enough not to move on to this particular organization.

EMPLOYABILITY

Harvard business professor Rosabeth Moss Kanter uses the word "employability" to mean much more than the ability to land a job. In *When Giants Learn to Dance,* Kanter defines "employability" as the ability to make *today's* work applicable to *future* opportunities.

If you're not acquiring new skills, that's a valid reason for leaving a job. Unless you're constantly updating your skills, you're falling behind. The jobs of the future will require a different set of skills than today's jobs. You need to be developing those skills now.

Also, before you take a job, don't limit your research to a company's website. Also go to Google, Bloomberg.com, Forbes.com, and other business websites. Otherwise, you may see nothing but a flurry of company press releases—which conveniently omit any mention of that irksome lawsuit or brewing CEO scandal.

GOOD-BYE TO THAT JOB

Switching from your present job to one that—at least in your eyes—is better is often cause for euphoria. That could be a premature reaction. First, you don't want to set yourself up for disappointment. After all, your new job might be great, but it will also inevitably be flawed. Second, boasting triumphantly about your new position will not endear you to your current colleagues.

Gloating is unwise because, first of all, you're setting up a me-against-them mentality. There you are, going off to this wonderful new position, while all those poor slobs are trapped in their same old jobs in the same old company. Second, it's inappropriate, because implicitly you're challenging the left-behinds to show some initiative and get a good job just like yours. Third, you might not be smiling for long.

Whatever the drawbacks of your current job may be, it also

holds a big advantage: You know it inside out. You know every detail involved in your job. You know the office culture. You know the personalities and the peculiarities of the key players. In the new job, for all you know, you may never be able to acquire the same knowledge base. The adjustment to your new job may be so difficult that you'd like to seek out the familiar—that is, people you know from the old job. Don't alienate them during the good-byes.

EXIT INTERVIEWS

Another sensitive issue is the exit interview. They're not confidential. Therefore, use your common sense. You don't want to say anything during an exit interview that could hurt your reputation or make you appear to be a crybaby. The purpose of the exit interview is to provide information to the organization about why people leave. More money, more responsibility, a shorter commute—all are conventionally acceptable reasons for leaving your job. Exit interviews were not created to be a form of therapy in which you vent your feelings about how the bosses and your colleagues did you wrong. Deliver that tirade, if you must, to your spouse, your best friend, or your diary. Keep it entirely out of the professional realm.

I always encourage young people to write a constructive letter to their ex-boss on the way out. It helps everyone.

BENEFITS AND COMPENSATION

Another important item you have to handle before leaving your current job is the state of your benefits and compensation.

It is crucial that you square away these items before you leave the company. Once you're no longer around, making these inquiries will be much more complicated, and don't imagine that someone at your old company will be happy to do it for you. It won't happen.

Find out when your health-care benefits become effective on the new job (human resources can tell you that). If there's a gap—perhaps your new benefits don't go into effect for several months—can you use your current benefits in the interim? The answer is usually yes. Even if you quit, the federal COBRA law allows you to extend your current coverage at the group rate. That way, you'll pay less than you would for an individual policy. If you don't sign up for COBRA, you can still be covered for sixty days if you pay the premiums retroactively. This means, in other words, that you don't have to stay in the old job just to hold on to your health care.

If you're close to being vested in the organization's pension plan, it might be financially worth your while to hang in there a little longer. That way, you'll get both your pension contribution and your employer's contribution. The wise thing—though not always the possible thing—is not to touch this nest egg. You can roll the whole amount over into your new employer's retirement plan or into an Individual Retirement Account (IRA). Consider consulting a financial planner about this.

You may have vacation days due you. If it's not yet bonus time, can you get a portion of that bonus when you leave, or will you receive the whole thing when the other bonuses are given out? Asking may be awkward, but you're well within your rights to do so. These are benefits you have earned.

YOU'RE IN CHARGE

In the new economy, you're in charge of your career. This chapter simply presents some guidelines. What's important is for *you* to take charge. Being passive leads nowhere. If you think it's time for you to move on, you have to be the one to initiate the move.

Things to Remember

- A job change is a serious decision
- There are valid and invalid reasons for a job change
- You're responsible for your own career

CONCLUSION

This chapter is must reading IF:

- You want to continue to be successful
- Everything around you keeps changing

Congratulations. You now know the ropes. You can graduate from boot camp. You can go out there and get what you want. You understand everything that it took my generation years to learn.

ALL ABOUT STRATEGY

Oh, you'll forget a lot of the details you read about in this book. You probably won't remember some of the characters on the grapevine, such as the "good mother." And you've probably already forgotten how many businesses go under in the first few years. But what you should have down cold is that in your professional life, you have to think strategically. Your career, your professional reputation, your promotions and pay raises—they're all about strategy.

For instance, you don't just access the grapevine in your office and start asking about Joe. Before you approach the grapevine you should have thought through: (a) Why are you asking about Joe? (b) Whom are you approaching about Joe? (c) What will this information about Joe "cost" you in terms of favors you'll owe? (d) What happens if Joe finds out that you've been asking about him? Every one of your actions at work can have multiple consequences. That's what you have to think about before you act.

You won't be successful, at least not for long, if you don't approach every aspect of your professional life on a strategic basis. That ranges from whom you befriend at work to how you manage your bosses when they have personal problems.

Smart pros—those who win in the workplace—think of their careers as businesses they're running. Their careers are as important to them as Amazon is to Jeff Bezos or Starbucks to Howard Schultz. You would be wise to approach your professional life in the same manner. That means that you ought to be as objective in your research and observations as possible. If something you are doing is hurting the business, then you have to look at that factor in your life. Suppose you're working in White Plains, a small city a few miles north of New York. You feel out of the loop and aren't meeting many colleagues from Manhattan. What are your options? Or you checked with headhunters and discovered that your compensation is below the average. Is that any way to run a business? What do you want to do about it?

You can no longer depend on the company or boss to look out for you. Your career is now entirely your business.

STRATEGIC PLANNING MEETINGS

At least once a week you must have a "strategic planning meeting" about your "business." You can conduct those "meetings" alone, by yourself. Or you can invite your mentor or friends to attend. You want to analyze where you've made progress that week and what your setbacks were. Are your original goals becoming outdated? For instance, maybe your goal was to become assistant manager in two years, but your organization has started to downsize. Maybe your new goal should be to survive for the time being or to hunt for another position in a more secure environment. Another aspect of cultivating your "business" is looking at your contacts. Is your circle getting bigger or smaller, and what is the quality of those contacts? In your inner circle should be some people who not only support but also challenge you and push you to be your best professional self. What new skills have you been learning? Are you bored?

BEING HAPPY

In your strategic planning sessions you also have to look at the emotional part of your life. Are you happy? Your happiness is as important to your success as the MBA you picked up or the new product you're working on in the design studio. Happy people, whether in organizations or self-employed, tend to get ahead.

Years ago at a telecommunications organization I met a man I'll call Dave. Dave did not have the typical profile for big success. He wasn't a tall, good-looking WASP; his ethnic origin classified him as a minority, and in those days members of his ethnic group were not exactly on the fast track at any organization. Dave's education was also atypical. He hadn't gone to a brand-name university full-time; instead, he had attended a local college in the evening. He had started his career with the organization in a blue-collar position, and it is usually difficult, if not impossible, to move from blue collar to white collar. Yet Dave rose, seeming effortlessly, to the upper tiers of the organization. Despite plenty of reorganizations, Dave is still there. And still walking the halls with a smile.

Over the years, we Dave-watchers analyzed his rise to leadership positions. We had to agree that Dave was no tiger like GE's Jack Welch. He wasn't brilliant in any particular area of business. His energy level was average. And, on his watch, mistakes had been made. So there were blemishes on his track record.

We came to attribute Dave's professional success to the fact that he was a happy person. People liked being around him. Since he wasn't bursting with resentments against the world and the organization, there was no chance that he would lash out at you. He was rarely if ever suspicious that various factions were out to get him, and that made him seem relaxed and intelligent. If attacked or challenged at a meeting, he calmly explained the facts. He seemed to see no value in holding a grudge. The people who worked for Dave loved him. Most of his superiors were interested in his doing well, so they would help him over the rough spots. Dave thrived. And is still thriving.

Go into your local department store and observe the young people who work at the counters. Some of them are happy doing what they're doing—at least for the time being—and some are not. Some are full of self-pity and will tell you, "I went to University X, and here I am, a salesclerk." I predict that those unhappy people won't move far from that counter. The happy people, on the other hand, make a good impression on you. You enjoy doing business with them. Some of those happy people will be selected by the store to become buyers and managers. Some of them will take the initiative to enroll in the Fashion Institute of Technology or take some business courses. Some might open their own store. For the unhappy people there's usually nowhere to move; they're blocked by their misery.

If you're not happy at work, find out why. And do something about it. Maybe you're in the wrong work environment. Maybe you're in the wrong profession. Maybe you're simply in the wrong city; you should be in L.A. instead of New York. The longer you're unhappy at work, the more your professional reputation will suffer. Unhappiness shows. And because it does, it has always been a career killer.

THE FIVE GOALS

In your strategic planning sessions you want to review the five goals we spoke about in the Introduction. Those five goals should be the "pull" force in your career. If you're not making progress toward those goals, your career is probably stalled.

1. *Gaining self-knowledge.* Self-knowledge is a moving target. As circumstances change, you will probably change, and you might have to get acquainted with yourself all over again. When I left corporate life and became an entrepreneur, I changed. I had to take the time to figure out who I was, what my priorities were, and what sacrifices I was willing to make for the business. My relationship with my wife also changed. I could no longer guarantee her a regular paycheck. My relationship with my children changed. I had to consider whether the risks I was taking in my own business might harm them. For instance, if I took a risk in dealing with Client X, and Client X dropped me and went to another agency, did that mean the children wouldn't be going to Disney World that year?

Every week, write down the ten things that are most important to you in work. Then write down the ten things that are most important in your personal life. Those lists should change over time. If they don't, either you're not growing, or you don't know who you are.

2. *Feeling empathy.* Whether you're firing a subordinate or congratulating a boss on her latest success, you have to assess how that person might feel. If you can learn to walk in that person's shoes, you will be successful in your career—and avoid those interpersonal disasters that sideline many a competent professional.

You can learn empathy by being in close touch with how you yourself feel. Suppose your boss just received a promotion. Conventional wisdom would have it that she should be elated. From your own experience with success, though, you know that a new victory can stir up a lot of old self-doubts. So you might want to reassure the boss that she's up to the new challenge. If the situation warrants, go heavier on the reassurance and lighter on the praise.

If you lack empathy, you're going to make plenty of interpersonal mistakes, and they always create havoc. You tell the person who just got laid off how rotten the job market is. You tell the person who just made assistant manager how much resentment there is in the company about the promotion. You tell the receptionist how bright he is and how he should get an education to get a better job. Eventually you're going to get kicked out of the organization or lose your business.

As you continue to check out how you're feeling about your work and your life, you will recognize that many in your professional circle probably have similar feelings.

3. *Presenting yourself well.* Often people make instant judgments about you based on very little information. No one understands this better than salespeople. Salespeople who make cold calls know that the outcome might rest on their tone of voice. If their tone doesn't hit the person called the right way, they've lost an opportunity.

Professionally, you will present yourself on the phone, on paper, in person, online, and in front of groups. How you present yourself in the workplace when you first get out of college will be different from how you present yourself when you're promoted to director. One of the biggest mistakes young people make is not realizing that they have to modify their image as circumstances change. As you gain more confidence and traction in an organization, for instance, you could become more low-key, less obviously eager to please.

When you don't reconfigure your image at the appropriate times, there's a discontinuity, and you create confusion. For instance, if you've become a manager of marketing, yet you're presenting yourself like a high school cheerleader, you will find that people might treat you as you appear, not according to your rank in the hierarchy. Organizations are filled with people who are going nowhere because they fail to recognize that they have to adjust their image as their circumstances change.

Every month look at yourself in the mirror. Look over the clothes in your closet. Does what you see represent who you are now? Listen to the way you speak. Do you over-explain things? Do you still sound like a kid, or is there authority in your tone? What does your body language say about who you are?

4. *Retrieving information effectively and being informed.* Being able to retrieve information is essential. Being informed is equally important. That encompasses everything from keeping up with the information on the grapevine to knowing what's happening in the news.

In the current work world, deficits in knowledge will be held against you. You should know what's going on in the world. You also should know how to read a balance sheet and what's happening in the stock market, even if these skills are not on your job description. And you should notice what skills your colleagues possess that you could acquire. Ask superiors and colleagues what you should be learning. If the majority of your peers are certified in insurance, maybe you should also become certified.

Regularly take an inventory of your skills and knowledge. Compare yourself to your peers. And remember that the more knowledgeable you are, the better your prospects are likely to be.

5. *Solving problems.* Your mantra should be, "Don't bring the bosses problems, bring them solutions." Whether you work for a multinational corporation or your own small business, you want a reputation as a problem-solver. I've seen capable professionals hurt their image by seeming overwhelmed by problems. Instead of solving the problems, they talk about them endlessly and confess their doubts about finding solutions. They wind up shaking other people's confidence in them.

Every week, review the problems in your personal and professional life. Get advice from someone you trust or ask yourself, "What would a top-notch problem solver do about these difficulties?"

Then judge whether it's time to implement a solution. Timing can be everything. Waiting too long because you hope a problem will disappear doesn't usually work, but jumping in precipitously can produce disasters. It's probably a truism that the time for anything is never really perfect. Still, if a problem isn't going away, sooner or later you will have to address it. So make a plan. That way, when the moment arrives, you will be prepared to take action. And if you make a mistake—well, so what? It happens to the best of us.

PLAYING TO WIN

Technology changes, administrations change, the economy changes. But beneath all that, life goes on pretty much the way it always has, and the road to success has not changed in millennia. That's why I take comfort in the meditations of Marcus Aurelius, the second-century Roman emperor who had an uncanny ability to put problems in perspective. "Do not be dilatory in action, muddled in communication, or vague in thought," he writes. "Don't let your mind settle into depression or elation."

Oh, and he adds one more thing: "Allow some leisure in your life."

Your future depends on it.

Things to Remember

- Career success means strategic thinking
- Happiness is a factor in success
- Pay attention to knowing yourself, developing empathy, presenting yourself effectively, gathering information, and solving problems

INDEX